LAST CHANCE

for the

TARZAN

HOLLER

Also by THYLIAS MOSS

POETRY

Hosiery Seams on a Bowlegged Woman

Pyramid of Bone

At Redbones

Rainbow Remnants in Rock Bottom Ghetto Sky

Small Congregations

MEMOIR

Tale of a Sky-Blue Dress

FOR CHILDREN

I Want to Be

LAST CHANCE

for the

TARZAN

HOLLER

POEMS
THYLIAS MOSS

Persea Books
New York

for Charlie
—Thanks.

Acknowledgments

Grateful acknowledgment is made to the following periodicals in which some of the poems in this volume (some in slightly different versions) previously appeared:

"In the Pit of Crinoline Ruffles" and "The Lighter Side of Shadows of Monsters" in *The Nation;* "Crystals" and "Ambition" in *Bellingham Review;* "Heads," "In the Right Empowerment of Light," and "After Reading *Beloved*" in *Michigan Quarterly Review;* "Accessible Heaven" and "The Limitation of Beautiful Recipes" in *Crab Orchard Review;* "In the Unholy Land of Sleep" in *Sycamore Review;* "Ant Farm" and "Hot Time in a Small Town," in *Kenyon Review;* "Beginning the Rock at Abbot School" and "A Way of Breathing" in *Callaloo;* "Advice," "First Grade Art: What Meets the Eye," and "Cheating" in *Solo.*

The author wishes to thank the John Simon Guggenheim Memorial Foundation and the John D. and Catherine T. MacArthur Foundation whose generous support made the writing of the this book possible.

Persea Books
171 Madison Avenue
New York, New York 10016

Library of Congress Cataloging-in-Publication Data
Moss, Thylias.
    Last chance for the Tarzan holler: poems / by Thylias Moss.
      p. cm.
    ISBN 0-89255-229-8 (alk. paper)
    I. Title.
PS3563.O8856L37   1998   97-24005
811'.54—dc21   CIP

Text designed by Rita and Robert Lascaro and typeset in Bembo with Bodoni titles.
Printed and bound by Haddon Craftsmen, Scranton, Pennsylvania

First Edition

There, under roots and in the medulla of the air,
erroneous things are understood as true.

—Federico García Lorca
(translated by Greg Simon
and Steven T. White)

What are we anyhow, we warmth-
hungry, breast-seeking animals?

—Amy Clampitt

Contents

Beauty, The Beast; Those Two 1

1—FIRE WORK

A Way of Breathing 5
In the Pit of Crinoline Ruffles 6
Beginning the Rock at Abbot School 7
Passing the Rock at the Phelps School 8
Those Who Love Bones 9
Juniper Tree of Knowledge 13
Last Chance for the Tarzan Holler 16
Ant Farm 21
Ambition 24
Ear 26
A Shoe in the Road 28
The Right Empowerment of Light 31
For Hagar 32
Crystals 34
A Hot Time in a Small Town 36
Glory 38
First Grade Art: What Meets the Eye 41
The Limitation of Beautiful Recipes 42

2—DARK EMBRACE

Second Grade Art: The Stunning Chances 47
A Walk Through the *Dark Embrace* 49
Easter 54
Heads 55
Tea Bags 56
Overseeing the Cherry 57

After Reading *Beloved*   59

In the Unholy Land of Sleep   60

A Man   61

Decision   63

The Saint and the Modern Equivalent of the Miracle of Lactation   65

Lines for a Wet Nurse   67

Saint Anthony's Ecstasy   68

Splitting a Double Life   70

Ode to the Cat-headed Consort in a Painting by Bosch   72

3—LUMINOUS LYMPH

Two Things   77

Those Immortal Axillary Animals   82

King Kong   84

Macaques Checking Each Other for Lice: A Public Display   85

Cheating   87

Sour Milk   90

Advice   99

Not Suffering   104

Accessible Heaven   107

EPILOGUE

The Lighter Side of Shadows of Monsters   111

NOTES   114

BEAUTY, THE BEAST;
THOSE TWO

A crush. The Beast releases
a tambourine from a mirror's strife

with skin of his own back, treble cleft
in the basso profundo's tense playback,

rewinding faster and faster
to Caruso's earliest recordings.

Hear the scratchy approach of brute,
sore throat becoming flute.

1
FIRE WORK

A WAY OF BREATHING

Playing jacks without hands, I'm no child
of Thalidomide but if I were would still show off:
Look Ma, no hands, no cavities.

Me and my Ipana smile are on my Schwinn,
the chain following its tight ellipse as my feet
pump rubber Popsicles to get in the jacks mood,
out of traffic, on the porch, cool drink nearby, shadow
of ferns like a crown. In fourth grade we learned
to dance on shoe prints in the gym, some girls with girls,
there were more of us, then we played jacks.

Jacks are asterisks, atoms, Sam Jaffe
on Ben Casey charting birth with chalk.
When you throw down jacks, you throw down
molecules; some spin.

Mouth can bounce a ball, lips
are rubbery anyway, especially liver lips,
the way they mold a wad of pâté,
or pancake Silly Putty over Sunday funnies,
lifting off punch lines; the lips say: pat-a-cake,
pat-a-cake, bake a man brittle so his arms fall off.

Follow the bouncing cherry
and sing along with me, Ipana, and Mitch.
A-one-and-a-two-and-a-three. I'm stuck
on onesies. A deep breath activates
both my Hoover: *jacks vacuumed*
up the nostril, one, two, three, four;
and some rebel: *jacks out the nostril,*
bang-bang, bang-bang.

IN THE PIT OF CRINOLINE RUFFLES

That spring there were cloth
t-strap shoes dyed to match
an egg-blue dress
deeper blue
in the pit of crinoline ruffles.

There was a starched cloth menu
that white curtains brushed
every time the breeze surged
and filled my cup.

In an apron of the same crinoline,
her hair like Marian Anderson's,
she took my order
and brought hot Maypo,
its curls of white steam
easing the tightness of her hair.

Always the black Singer laid
its own crinoline tracks across
peaks and gullies, difficult domestic
terrain, and sickness
until the house was full
of crinoline epiphany.

She sat wrapped in it too,
and standing seemed to rise
from stiff mist, the egg-blue dress
finished, a mantle over her arm, lace
and pearly buttons, satin sash, her wages,
the shroud of Golgotha restored.

My hat had a brim wide as Saturn,
hers was earthbound, no brim at all.

After sunrise service, she walked
all the way to Saturn whose rings
dropped round my waist
to take me home. But first
          I danced for her.

BEGINNING THE ROCK AT ABBOT SCHOOL

It's the sixties and it's okay because *the rock hits my forehead*
like my grandmother's hand: blunt love. What it was
was the laying down of law and never was it messy although

the law was laid because of messes I'd made. Say it was Saturday
and I was shaking the booty as if that was the reason I was born;
her hand fixed my future that I had no business shaking, upsetting

transistors, killing receptors; we had to hear static all night. I could
shatter papier-mâché-wrapped light bulbs to provide access to maracas
so that it was a festive rut I faced no matter which direction I turned.

My feverish anger rose and rose until it hit this hand that went *smack*,
that went *whap*. Hey, hey, now; in my hand I've got the vertebra
that held her up when pride failed, then she fell, leaning to reach something,

beyond my seeing her again. But here's the link leaned towards
in my hand, my fingers closing around nugget as if it could fly away: this
heaviness, this weight, this presence, this memory.

It might be a piece of Galileo's brain, anatomical synopsis. I think
we are born with a piece of that brain, piece of that dreaming, piece
of that wondering. I think that we each

submit to gravity again and again.

PASSING THE ROCK AT THE PHELPS SCHOOL

From the right you lucky piece of gneiss, striated like bacon,
hardened like arteries, you granite white with feldspar, you chalk,
talc, and chert—you protozoan cemetery, you entomologic impostor,
so much in you wants to be mealy bug, you old speckled devil, saboteur
of that John Deere, you savior of soulless grass.

From the right you haphazard skull mimic,
no brain ever so small as to honor you,
you hardly head, limestone dome, you unfit bone

shattered into everlasting stream from my right, you bowl of old trail mix,
unbowled bowl of peas, pills, pellets, and turds, you abject fossils, gonads
and tonsils strong but petrified that the past might pass away, you excavated mime,
duty placed in my hand, you fibroid, old, old money, you sedentary example
ripe for martyrdom—I pass thee to David, the igneous fault is thine.

THOSE WHO LOVE BONES

1.
Wilma's hair, stringy red meat, bone fixed
vs. Scarlett's corsets, exoskeletons—

not so much bone
as dust

2.
No contest—She loved bones more (her name
won't help), common woman, common problem, didn't do anything
but love to get at the bare bones of it all, ribs, for instance,
of the ark, splendid up-turned curves, thin as digits of corpses
breaking through the crust, available for complete rescue; how she loved

them, slept once with her cheek pressing on his, trying to crush his, grind his,
next best thing to rhino horn, aphrodisiac that made Wendy fly when Peter
sprinkled it on her.

3.
Sometimes, she didn't need him
because beneath her flesh, so excessive
at all the creases it folded over like Jack-in-the-pulpit,
plant-of-peace whose arum reminds those who see it
that it's time to copulate so it's banned
from the altar, were her own

bones.   Schoolboys

bite into Jack's corm, as fleshy as a woman
of experience, and thereafter call it memory-root;
they're not likely to forget the acridity, the woman's refusal.
        There is needle-like calcium oxalate
in the root, effects of pepper on the tongue
before it burns so badly not another grace will be said
that day.

With the burn comes *the most pure*
and white starch that bludgeoned her hands
when she set it to laundry; she nearly got to the bone.
Her customers' necks blistered from treated collars.

She loved bones, stewed neckbones slowly
so the meat would fall off, leaving liberated vertebrae
in the pan like dice (a.k.a. bones) with holes punched out;
she sucked them for hours, would not answer the phone
or rush so quickly to her feet that the rhythm of sucking
would be disrupted.   Loved to dig them up

4.
from the fat breast of capon, to contemplate the archaeology
that could happen if in the barnyard, poultry had scratched up
old teeth and swallowed them like grain; she hadn't yet found
canines or incisors in the carcass on her plate, white napkin
across her lap as if it was time for gynecology, but remained dedicated
to blackened, rounded bones from thighs, legs, the ends
just like knuckles tapped for sweetness when she sucked
making up for what didn't happen when she was born.
She loved bones best
                              when they were cleaned, varnished, dried,
a complete skeleton of a flounder displayed like a harp.
She loved the skeleton of Joseph Merrick but not as much
as the bony pop star who reportedly wanted to purchase it
for a million dollars from a museum of human remains
at the Royal London College of Medicine. Merrick's bones
had been boiled once already
so they could be mounted.   Proteus syndrome,
some say; the pop star
has another.

She loved bones so much she vigorously rubbed wrinkle cream
into her face so she could feel her cheekbones, but this did nothing
for progesterone and estrogen's monthly crop of white-heads, white spots
like those that killed all the pimelodellas in the fish tank; or could be eczema,
ordinary papules, but given the wasting

syndrome she volunteers to see, hospice 1996, soon the bones
will be on the table
and they will tell everything; they're such suckers
for forensic medicine.

Even after long silences   they may be exhumed
and even if the surviving fragment is just a piece of skullcap
no bigger than a nicotine patch, William Maples

still can tell how alligators gnawed it at the bottom
of a river two years after the hatchet man put it there; there's
a bible of bones in a barn in the former Yugoslavia

5.
and thick as grief around Pol Pot's feet. Pray for these anchors,
pray for *the hamfat man's* lowered minstrel standard
to celebrate the awkwardness of problem bones   on Merrick's right
side as if his share of a black mama's unlimited access to blight,
her compulsory burden to oppose the elegant left(over)'s
classic countenance; he got a good sinistrous limb (pity not a good foot)
from that miscegenetic split personality, rapture of Canaan seceding
from the cedars of Lebanon, wheat from chaff, privilege from his walking
like Hambone who's palsied, demented and living on the streets, used
to love somebody long gone.   *Hey, Hambone; Hey, Daddy* she calls as

he passes, as she sits there sucking those tasty hard things
without a bone to pick with anyone: no whalebone, ivory, no
Hambone in a hurry
to meet bones assembling in the valley for Jason and Ezekiel,
sowed teeth giving rise to armed skeletons pushing up
like botanical freaks, beanstalks, the bones pulling themselves
together until a million march on the day of the dead wearing
turbans and hives, turbans and hives
to help him win back his sweetheart.   *Hey, Honey.*

She stirs a big old pot with a long bone
all indigo to the level of the dye, a liquid muscle
rushes madly in a circle, writing (with the superb ink
of her belief) that those who love bones prevail
after waiting for flesh, weaker by the hour, to give way

to Bones: simple rhythm instrument, two parts
held between the fingers of one hand and clacked together. She'd love
for him to play bones for her, just for her. *Hambone, please
love the one you're with.   Don't end up*

6.
making castanets from a skull as did the Hatchet Man
who was later convicted, but somewhere out there

are castanets that aren't really castanets.

Somewhere out there also: catacombs, decay, decay, half-
lives, promises, a finger on a string to help a more perfect knot
come into being   on Wilma's wedding day, marriage to bone,
faithful, uncompromising truthful bone
                              —the mind cheats, soft
and dreaming, inventing words bone can't say, not even a simple
forensics-defying word: *race.*

JUNIPER TREE OF KNOWLEDGE

A wife prayed for a baby as she peeled an apple
under a juniper tree and cut her finger, the sight of blood
confirming she was not pregnant.

But she was, as if the tree gave her a little something-something
for feeding its roots her blood (rewards are also meted out
by the alien plant in *Little Shop of Horrors*).

Perfection: A tree, an apple, a husband to tell of her desire
to procreate, her knowledge of her readiness. No surprises
until the sight of her baby is so magnificent it kills her.

She's buried, as she wanted, under the tree, where the oil
of the juniper preserves her body. Underground
she grows lovelier, her beauty becomes so strong it seems
destined to return although it doesn't; this loss is real.

There is not a widower in the woods for long. Rustling leaves make
him long for skirts rustling as they lift to permit consummation. He
marries a woman well-past first apples; she has a daughter to be sister
to her new step-son who has the qualities best

in a young woman who because of them can climb
from echelon to echelon (as wife): red as blood, white as snow.
He seems too perfect to have a father, certainly does not
need a mother. She calls the death of his mother *matricide*.

The boy is in her way, interferes with her transformation
of shrine to *her* home, *her* herbs altering the air, *her* curtains
filtering the light, *her* spinning wheel hypnotizing
the new family into forgetting the old. She must assert

her touches. But that is not enough. Somehow women will resort
to apples. This woman has a chest of them, result of days and days
of gathering until the smell of the stages of ripening and rot
overtakes the cottage. It makes the step-son forget

his step-mother's resentment and diurnal refusal to give him an apple
when he comes home from school. The apple trees are all
picked clean; he's at the mercy of her merciless stash. This day
he forgets that generosity from her is a warning; *of course*

you can have an apple; help yourself. Then the lid of the apple chest
decapitates him. For a moment the step-mother just looks
and admires the success of that old hunger: the power of *Winesap,
Macintosh, Jonathan* hers to pull down with a slot machine lever:
jackpot, jackpot, jackpot.
There's no bleeding (and that's just more luck).

This can be explained.
She positions the body at the table, applies a little mortar to the neck
and fixes the head upon it, ties a silk scarf around the neat scar
and waits for her daughter to come home and ask (hasn't yet missed a day)
to give her brother an apple; she loves him deeply
so does not question her mother's miraculous permission.
Thinking the apple will be a welcomed first gift

Marie is distressed that the dead boy refuses it; it's good enough; she's
good enough, and she follows her mother's advice to slap him
if he refuses again, to kingdom come. Obedience: his head
falls to the floor, and her guilt flies everywhere. She's killed her brother
and her father's delight, everything is promised to him
and she's no fit alternative although politeness falls from her tongue
as if nothing else is there; she never says but that she killed him

and how wrong she was even if his had been a tyrannical presence
—no other boy had no lust at all. As mothers must, this one helps
her daughter; no body, no murder; no murder, no punishment.

                    They make soup

and serve the father heaping bowls of John. He slurps and tosses finger bones
and cuneiform bones of the foot under the table. Such tender meat. Not what the kings
and gods eat, but the kings and gods in the pot. In no time, tibia, femur, and plate cleaned
to make room for a wink at his new wife who has caught and skinned a bear. He'll boast
of that and all will be afraid to ever challenge either one of them; she caught a bear
and he caught her. John soup is the best soup he's ever had. She can cook too.

More, more

and soon his wife licks the spoon, her only and the last taste. He ate it all. Marie rocks
the bones under the table, kisses phalanges, and they do taste good, how can they taste good?
So much crying she seems to make more soup. *It is good enough to make you cry*
Father agrees. Finally: *Where's John?* Working, studying, visiting
his sick aunt, seeking his fortune, becoming a man—any one or all of these.

Marie wraps the bones in silk and drags them to the juniper tree, buries them one
by one, loves John more than ever, his bones dazzling in moonlight,
each one a wand. She writes his name in the air and it stays there, insects
holding it in place; she reads it in the clear ink of sudden rain inscribing her face,
and it's the message in the slime trail of snails—juniper branches
sign it, wind weeps it, feathers dry it and the bird begins the next day

singing about a step-mother who's wife and self-taught butcher, who's framing
her own daughter for the homicide, and feeding her own step-son to his father.
What a catchy song, no other bird has sung it; it speaks of indecency but with such
sweetness—impossible, but they hear it; all who hear it sing it too, finding they know it
by heart instantly; all its harassment, intolerableness, and beauty

that they follow to the cottage where the bird first acknowledges innocence
with a gold chain for the father and red shoes for Marie that teach her
how to dance again, then the step-mother, trying to run from the burning house
that is her own skin, is greeted with a millstone the bird drops, the sweetness aching
to break her neck, fracture her skull, and make her food

for the condors and vultures. Marie and Father watch them eat
(the miracle is not over), joined by John who's resurrected in time for supper
that Marie rushes to fix; she has no time for grief, and the vultures
have done such a good job anyway of making grief unnecessary.

LAST CHANCE FOR THE TARZAN HOLLER

1. The season that precedes Dali's *Autumn Cannibalism*

This day, like all days,
is a day of reckoning.

Gretel has felt electricity before
while rebaking walls and repairing
the licorice roof, scraping mold

off the stale door
of the loaf in which she rooms
since inheriting the bread house

from the one who died there; her
assistance with the suicide assists
her cruelty.   Humperdinck's
Rubylips, witch, bitch ≈ Gretel, baker, widower-maker

G is the mature audience
for the scene of the crime
of comfort in this warm chair

warm as a living thing.
Ruby warming herself
in the stove.

The end.
Aw; tell me more, Mommie,
dearest Medea.

2. Unity, Inc.

This time perhaps the current will follow the blue path
          of veins in arms cuffed in leather. Loop-the-loop, the
Rotor, amusement park centrifugal thrill, Blue Streak, once
          a monster coaster. Wet and Wild's giant water slide, big
splash of grief into Dali's *Premonition of Civil War,*

accurate although war can not be suave, gracious, or able
to partake of Susan Smith's southern hospitality. Civil(ity).

Anguish has no edge: entrails, body parts, Ruby's ashes,
bones that remain rounded for everlasting womanhood,
bombs for which bare-breasted women modeled; anguish
is a *soft construction with boiled beans,* soft as kindness, soft
boys: Michael and Alex, strapped in safety seats like the one
in my car, a Century 2000 on which is written:
for the safety and comfort of Ansted Moss.
Every morning he recites this scripture
as we drive past a transformer, farms, the Huron River.

One of Susan's soft-lipped boys plunged
at the age I was for my first baptism, naked
under the white robe and not aware
of how much of my wet self
the preacher's hand covered. He was holy
and I was becoming that way.   Last chance
for the Tarzan holler. Those boys too

are believers. Everyone believes something.
Susan Smith will get better, believe it or not.
Premonition of amnesia. She's not alone,

practitioners of Munchausen's syndrome by proxy
feed off sympathy for the sometimes fatal, dreamed up
pathologies of their children; does turned vixen maintained
by salt licks through winter until it is the season to hunt
them down like dogs with dogs, like dogs eating dogs
until they're all gone in a premonition of peace; no
more best friends, nepotism, parricide.   She's

not alone. Accompanies those heading
for abortion clinics. These

madnesses, these choices, a little off
the top versus complete make-over, back
to the drawing board of unlimited ideas
where Medea, Gretel are born. It is that easy.
I see everyone at the market, everyone at

the clinic. And they see me. It is
that necessary. Breathe
a little easier for ten minutes

then the Mazda sinks.

—Cells, those drawings torn
out of animated existence are cels; how
I hate homonymity, as if I am singularly composed
of wicked artistry.

3.   Knock, knock.
       Who's there?
       Marrow.
       Whose marrow?

Zaynah is a girl whose match of bone marrow
may depend on boys dead in the water.

Her father loves her without this maudlin push
but after the press conference many others love her too,
including, he hopes, he pleads, the woman who adopted
Zaynah's first cousins when for their safety and comfort
they were removed from risk, maternal as that risk was;
they may be the bearers of the soft, fatty, vascular interior
of bones, collaborators in a life blood-postulated.

Gretel's wicked matriarchy.

       Knock, Knock.
       Come in, says the oven.
       But you don't even know who's there!
       Doesn't matter.
       Ah, a paragon of equal opportunity.

In that other house of bread where deacons serve it
all cut up, there is after the light one
a heavy supper of beans, squash, and pork chops.

The cooks sit hot in folding chairs by doors
and windows propped open with hymnals, and suck
a sweet intensity
from well-blackened bones of swine.

There is nothing between life and death, solid
and liquid forms of equivalent sacredness. Between
us, grudges.
                    Just like *that!*
you're in John D. Long Lake
that does not know a day in which light
does not skim it like a wing,

especially on the October day that a car,
though a chariot is preferred, released two boys,
spirit willing, from their bodies so they could

sink into homecoming, alive
in comfortable seats
that can withstand collisions at 50 mph
if fastened properly—as they were. Susan's

marrow is eligible; Zaynah's life
could depend on the charity of the one
whose marrow is innocent, who did not put
her hands on her own marrow, did
not masturbate, was molested
although, knock, knock, these days
who wasn't?

Susan, I don't mean to be cruel
but as you know it is inevitable. She

once took the boys on a picnic near water
cool and effervescing with motherhood
that blew bubbles that emerged
from Michael's right ear when she whispered
in his left, a rummage

of secret disappointments in school, so much
to remember, fix; life imprisoned in ego. Susan

likes Mr. Quixotic, *psst, pass it on*—*does not*—*does too*
and wants the time of day from shrugging shoulders,
silhouette

like iron monument in the park. They date
in her dreams and she's the Florence Nightingale
of Hadleyville and Roanoke that someone—Michael
(her son or the angel?)—said she couldn't be, kissing
away hurt until her lips rot

with duty and her ankles swell into cast iron casts,
weighing her down with identity—who did she marry?
Why isn't the love of her new life here under
bandages that she, the Arachne of Hadleyville and Roanoke,
wrapped into parcel, care package saved
for all the rainy days it takes to make a lake?

She kept her eyes on the loophole
in her wedding ring, so where's her Houdini?

Talcum and corn starch fill the air
as Gretel flails trying to escape a bathtub
turned to pudding, trying to escape

the revenge of marrow.

ANT FARM

One summer day
I took a kettle of steaming water and flooded an ant hill, watched as balled black bodies
floated down my brewed Nile and dried in the sand looking sugared, cinnamon-crusted.
I should have baked them into cookies and become famous for indecipherable
irresistible taste, a certain *je ne sais quoi*. Or thought to serve them poached. This
annihilation was not annihilation; the ants did not suffer and were turned into sugar beads
and their floating was serene.   I didn't know there'd be few

survivors; I expected in insects stamina a backbone obfuscates,
keeping vertebrates upright and vulnerable, subject to arrogance, breakage,
ravages, paralysis, the ideal immobility of food, facilitating admonishments to eat
until bones are picked clean, not only piranhas eating their instinct, but families
in public: Red Lobster, Bill Knapps, Kentucky Fried, countless rib joints, clean
as ivory; meals conclude with skeletons.   I admire teeth, the cutting

of the first one long before there can be any controlling of the bowels, a first pair
center front, vegetarian before that fulfillment; meat's indigestible until the fontanels
seal fate. Fetus eats as if entirely an embryonic flower, through root and stem called cord.
In the slits fanning around the navel like the possibility of petals
are dark slivers reminiscent of ants without their legs and my first boyfriend's
delight.   I killed them

although I had an ant farm sitting by my bed, such a narrow world it was, pressed between
sheets of Plexiglas no bigger than standard issue composition paper on which
I took notes on their progress that in my notebook never was, for I kept looking
at them from my perspective had I been as restricted; they could not open the world, reach
for stars though their tunnels longed to be telescopes.
Could not use a mirror's condolences to double their impression of space, so busy, busy,
carrying on their drudgery to distract them from escaping, even an ant queen
who could not fly away to mate with a marked man, but one day, her wings

were discarded, as they should be after the nuptials, at the opening to a tunnel, like a set
of tiny lips, white such as what, at the time, I thought happened, the bleaching, if arsenic
was kissed, but it happens too when there's too much confectioner's sugar
on what is consumed, and usually, when consumption takes place, there's too much
something, what, of course, varies so that sooner or later, everything has a turn being vice.
Outside, trophallaxis keeps ants going, reciprocal feeding, exchange of chemical

stimulation, workers (wingless, infertile females denied or uninterested in sex) tend
the young, feeding them honeydew from raids on aphids and giving other luscious stuff
of their own feeding to larvae whose surfaces secrete a substance more luscious that
these females crave, and thus, work even harder for the high, the all-consuming high,
the paradisiacal reward although these busy ants are neither saved nor unsaved nor
concerned. A group of lactating women assemble in a suburban park, get high together as
their babies nurse. Feelings some of them

don't get from spousal intimacy. Some fancy ants are living honey pots, workers,
through whatever awareness is possible in formic nervous systems, who know themselves
sublime as they are fed unbearable quantities of honeydew, and they must wonder whether
or not they are deserving of overwhelming pleasure though none complain, accepting a
blessed fate that nevertheless restricts their options. Then these females, rather ideally
nunnish, gorged to a real inedia, lose their ant form, becoming butterballs round as the
cosmos and becoming the cherubic sustainers of the colony, releasing sweet drops as
needed yet remaining full, complete. Diva ants.

The boyfriend who lived near water let ants crawl along his arms, then he would flick them
off, quickly kicking his leg, trying to catch them in his pants cuff. He became good
at this. Too good to forget.

There are close to five thousand species of ants, among them the Cameroonian
stink ant capable of producing a sound audible to humans, especially to women
full of milk who are so sensitive to crying, a frail decibel makes milk flow just as our
desperation is supposed to touch God to the point that he can't help but dispense remedies,
sometimes in code, to what has become his own misery. The stink ant feeds from the rain
forest floor and in just trying to survive, which is when everything happens, during
attempts at survival, sometimes inhales a fungal spore that survives in the ant's brain,
reproducing and controlling, using the ant as its slave wagon for transport to
            prominence
at the top of a fern, a pinnacle like a spear and the ant that knows of its disgrace,
despite the take-over of its brain, clamps its mandibles to the spear so that it seems
impaled, sort of an act of hara-kiri, and dies as the spore now flourishes, consuming
the totality of the dead meat; death graciously allows for less grievous consumption, more
open relish, and in two weeks, the time it takes for a woman to miss a period after
fertilization, a spike with a tip orange as sunset begins to emanate
from the former head of the ant, and upon reaching an inch and a half of success,
triggers fireworks, an explosion of spores descending from the heights and looking

for a sponsor.   There's an ant like this in Florida where you could be in love, foolish,
getting pregnant in grass on which some of these dead ants are fastened by their jaws.
I was told not to eat watermelon seeds, that vines and snakes would grow within me, so
after eating them, I took Castoria, the whole bottle of that gentle laxative for children,
although I knew, for the color betrayed it, that Castoria was made by liquefying ants, that
ants were farmed just to purge.

AMBITION

A boy says his father wants to be a Smurf
and no one can top that; no one else there has
ambition that comes close to that. Only his father
wants to be a Smurf.

His mother holds her shock still; no teen marriage here,
there was long engagement and shacking up long
before the license; she knew what was necessary to know
about this man: His lack of criminal past, his dislike
of physical solutions, the cycles of his preferences
that she has matched with three wardrobes and wigs.
This, however, he kept from her, would share only with
a son, his deepest desire his sex with her won't betray
in an elfin blue boundary. With her he is in love;
with the Smurf, he is deeper in himself.

Any moment could bring loss of anything. She is prepared
for theft of his heart by, she'd like to think, another woman,
or even better, a vehicular finishing by bus, car, truck, plane,
Harley, yacht or Hummer. A random act of God comforts.
Even fantasy can be robber.

Falling in love is not something done once then
the ability forsaken; part of what brought them together
was the time of morning, their vulnerability
when something so bright was starting, warming them
separately and together. So far, morning has arrived every day
and he could again be with a stranger when the sun
is at that identical angle that made him notice he wasn't alone.

Not that there need be hierarchy of loss, but the worst to her
is his new pride originating from his manhood, not from
the hermaphroditic entity that results from the influence
of marriage; a masculine, feminine merger that frightens
in its disrespect of boundaries on which order depends.
He is a man thoroughly, she notices, as he fingers
his Adam's apple; his face will not stay smooth, the beard invincible
even as it forfeits jet for a white haunting of masculinity he enjoys,
now praises wondering how he could love anything unlike this

and why he did not date the bearded lady he spent
all his quarters on; at least then he'd know
what the influence of beard is in a kiss.

It's more than that now; emptied of infatuation, left with
the aftermath of youth, it's beard he loves and testicle
and he wants the world to know of his epiphany, but still ruled
by fairness, first he tells his wife who's been hurt by impotence,
hurt by endometriosis, hurt by infertility, and the promises technology
can't make fast enough to help her, the cracking open of her own genes,
their reorganization while she's under general anesthetic sleeping
a hundred years, waking alone too old for a life
hers only through science. It's beard he loves and testicle.

Who knows what logically follows Smurf
even knowing the logic of arriving at Smurf?   Blue
as if offspring of a sky at last inspired as it has been inspiring.
Theirs is genealogy shared with Tinker Bell; indeed,
they have never tasted meat and are considered delicacy
by the animated villain who has never tasted Smurf,
not even a cool blue lick.

Never mind her injury; look at the benefit for the child
she knows she'll keep. He has never felt more pride,
more connection to his father.   No more doubting paternal love
now that the father wants his identity based on
something the son understands.

EAR

It is called the incomplete human flower, I know because I have called it that,
usually right before sex, when everything looks good. *You keep bringing me flowers,*
my tongue says sliding into the fossae of his right ear's helix and anti-helix
shown at left without my tongue.

Lacking one of those pretty and slim proboscides of certain avuncular bugs
(you know, the men keeping company with never-married mamas, too familiar
not to have a family title but most definitely not anybody's fathers) cruising
the flower beds needing a dose of hepatica or burst of the stench of rotting fish
and burnt sugar that the eight-feet tall lily *Amorphophallus titanum* of the Sumatran
jungle emits in a strength to knock a man flat out and take from carrion beetles
that last drop of resistance that was their whole blood, I can't get in

the internal ear's labyrinth, neither the osseous nor the membranous labyrinth
within the other, yet here is where sound happens, where that which means
to be heard must travel vestibule, canals, and cochlea to the mecca
of the auditory nerve. The body is nothing but tunnels, made for excavation, covert opera-
tions, ergo my tongue, this ear I want to pluck and pin to my lapel, wear it
as well as he does; no, better and both of them, one to wear above, beside, on

each breast, and he could speak right in them somehow speaking to all of me
of Calvoli Island where gulls, of the western point, kitsch their nests with:
bones, feces, regurgitated seafood, dead chicks and addled eggs and the gratitude
of blowflies accepting such lavish invitation to flourish, prosper.
Pampered they are indeed (as is this ear), and giddy, as gull excrement and stink
compete with putrescence of a flower, *Helicodiceros muscivorus,* an arum lily
presenting, for the blowflies' pleasure, a spathe color of decomposing meat and just
as fetid as *a well-matured sheep-sized corpse* so that

it's no contest; arum and blowflies have the orgy, flies pursuing *a dark, damp*
and particularly fetid aperture with which to mate, and that exists within the lily's
dark chamber past the neck and spadix, a space from which the flies do not escape,
the presence ilking up with humidity, rot-based arousal such as never known,
causing eggs to erupt from those places lust-distended on the insects, ova offered
for these services instead of cash, piling up as if a stripper has been fully plastered
with green. Naturally, maggots hatch, such is the intensity and odor, but perish without
real meat, real decomposition although for the parents, there is nectar of the flower
besides nectar of their erotic throes, and they are helpless to it, suck it up without
the howling my man likes to hear from me as a continuously updated status report

on his work. The morning after or morning after that, male flowers
give the pollen bath that releases those flies that have not suffocated
to *Sardinian sunlight* bright as approval so into the next lily inflorescence they rush
before this palace is shut down by an agricultural vice squad

just as sometimes he is deaf to all but Dow Jones, NASDAQ,
the numbers getting in deep, but I can add, multiply, divide and divide endlessly;
I can fuck with the numbers.

A SHOE IN THE ROAD

On some days, there are shoes in the road, not
pairs, but singles, this morning a white pump
soiled, leather peeling from the heel.

It lay near a brick that unlike the shoe
seemed to have had no encounters with misery.
Nowhere was it chipped and its porous surface

was filling rapidly with light
somehow suggesting the most glorious day
of the Aztecs, the day when it still seemed possible

that gods and infinity could be touched
beneath Spanish helmets.

The brick crushed its throne of fairly new
roadside grass whereas asphalt under the pump
gave no sign of yielding to any presences, the weight

of vehicles had yet to make a dent, no discoloration
from birds and spills, or the beginnings of erosion
though each day, there is a wearing away, even of myself,

each day a loss of dead cells and annoyances although most
of these are replaced (even pearls know miserable hearts,
the luster clasps remorse), but the wearing down of resistance

is relentless and is a movement towards revelation
of what is concealed by all this. I'm thinking the shoe
is the start of this trail: shoe here, wallet miles away, purse

in a drainage ditch, her whereabouts unknown, missing,
presumed to have disappeared like the subtle act of minutes
becoming years and regret, unnoticed because of the good

fraud of tomorrow; scarf caught on a rudder in Vancouver,
carried there the way good intentions, balloons, messages
and medicines in bottles can span incredible odds and distances,

germs and fragrances hitchhike in water, air, hopeful
as gyroscopes, and claim the world, global links triggered
by practically nothing at all: a shoe in the road

that fell from a bag hastily packed as a woman who hadn't
in years but believed one evening would again dance, fled
a brutality increasingly possible to imagine

behind game show doors and car doors, all doors
or that hit the road falling from a mishandled generosity
when it wasn't loaded well on the charity's blue truck

—still there was something contrary to aggression
behind the gesture although this shoe probably
won't be the one helping someone recover fox trots

that used to make her feel courageous enough
to endorse only frivolity—trumpets, drums, piano, and
trombones defying seriousness and contemplation,

forgetting the pending judgment, stalling
the coming sickness, halting the malicious necessity
for armor or even bones, so that she could move

in that gown like jellyfish or simpler plankton
and diatoms, with lean sparkle, sheer glimmer
that every teaspoon of ocean contains and that nets

leave behind, because the fishing and seeking
are for substance, what I finally demand of that shoe:
that it plug an emptiness underneath it,

that if I should pick it up, it will be real, real, more
reliable than my hand: digit, knuckle, cuticle,
thumb, metacarpal, lifeline, nails—a hand

is made of threats and complications. The pump
is today's masking tape and bandage,
is an alembic in which a series of thuds

as fearless as judgment, in which a stalker's bright,
quick clacks of the heel on concrete become
a tap dance's flurried finale, become

like injury or defect, a ritual
clumsiness that solicits rain
and every other mercy.

—for Betty who called it courage

THE RIGHT EMPOWERMENT OF LIGHT

In the right empowerment of light, pictures taken
are so well washed I get 4 x 6-inch rectangles
of light's domination.

In a photo of rural Japanese radishes that light finishes
with translucence, vegetables become slender lanterns
destined to appear as specialty of the house, but how to serve
the light, how to slice it; how to bite it, swallow it
without the chest lighting up, ribs becoming frame
for a lamp shade?
In church you chew on His death; you don't sample
His infinity.   What is the etiquette?

In the film about the infant emperor
the royal feces was collected in brass
jade and gold
and gave off light
in the kingdom so there was no opposition
to the production of milk by his wet nurse
for his lifetime that gave off light
in the beam of piss that in the sand
formed veins of gold.

I want to say it's radioactive: that last summer,
his sisters in the house first time in years,
I walked into the room rebellion with me
yet my father lit up, they said.

There is divine light.
There is also arrogance, the other
radiance.

FOR HAGAR

Children come from God, even Hagar's son Ishmael who was conceived with Abram,
husband of Sarai to whom Hagar was Egyptian slave, at Sarai's urging since
she herself was barren and pushing eighty. Hagar was the first surrogate mother, a maid, who
was alluring anyway and needed little persuading (she'd made goo-goo eyes at Abram
before) was offered to her mistress' husband as his concubine so that the mistress could have
a product of her husband's bloodline, the bloodline that mattered. Sarai held onto her
deeply-seeded hope that Hagar also was barren, so didn't get to hold that baby that she hated
Hagar for conceiving and then boasting of the conception, a vanity
to be reserved for the mistress of a household; Sarai snubbed her, treated her harshly
to keep Hagar submissive. But Hagar leaned, exaggerated how swaybacked the growing child
made her so that the pregnancy was more profound. The gorgeous belly. The belly dancing
that made mousy Sarai more mouse than ever, mini mouse, her little bombs had the effect
only of turds; Hagar swept them away with a prideful glance.
I've got this world, Hagar said, rubbing it.

Did Hagar not have Abram eating from her hands as well as from her thighs?

How she intended to disparage Sarai, believing Sarai would never conceive, would always be
subordinate to Hagar's fertility; Hagar believed she could be prolific at this, believed Abram
would want her to be prolific at this. *I count for nothing in her eyes,* said Sarai seeing Hagar
assume rank and power. The authority of a belly. Whale will swallow Jonah; Hagar swallows
the whale before it gets the chance. Hunger leads to this! Always be hungry. However, what
slave does not flee persecution even if her attitude has been haughty, satisfying, Abram
comfortable with non-procreative kisses?

*The angel of Yahweh met [Hagar] near a spring in the wilderness, the spring that is on the
road to Shur... The angel of Yahweh said to her, "...You will bear a son...A wild ass of a man
he will be, against every man, and every man against him, setting himself to defy all his
brothers."* Better than no contract between God and her son at all. And defiance
sounds better than submission. *I'm back, Sarai, and ordained. Here*

is an inter-racial child, the famous call-him-Ishmael, Abram's first born, the heir supreme, but
not the one that God wants as beneficiary of His covenant; no; that has been reserved for a
second child that God permits the ninety-year-old Sarah to have (He changes her name and
changes Abram's to "Abraham," exalting them above past infidelity; it wasn't us, they can
say, but Sarai and Abram who cheated), child of more certain ethnicity, pure-bred, not one of
those mulatto bastards of many new-world masters. But as Ishmael is a legitimate (meaning
authentic) son of God's chosen, he also must be blessed, just not as lavishly as his half-
brother Isaac; there will be some sort of affirming action; God says:

I will…make [Ishmael] fruitful and multiply him exceedingly; he shall be the father of twelve princes, and I will make him a great nation. But I will establish my covenant with Isaac. In this way does God establish a legal precedent for Rebekah

when she helps Jacob deceive his father Isaac, procuring for him the blessing meant for Esau (who has already sold his birthright to Jacob), the firstborn, just as that covenant should have been with Ishmael, the firstborn of Abram.
Once Sarah has a child of her own, a little smugness and revenge come upon her, the return of estrogen. Rich as she now is, she can afford some disdain for Hagar who has slept with her husband (at her request) and beaten Sarah to the conception punch. But as the sugar settles, Sarah finds her tardy swig sweeter, and under this influence, wants no rivals for her son Isaac. Ishmael, with that Egyptian glowing within him, his adolescence about to burst forth, oiled black panther, makes the celibate feel foolish. Sarah to keep her victory victorious, says to Abraham matter-of-factly: *Cast out this slave woman with her son; for the son of this slave woman shall not be heir with my son Isaac.*

God has no problem with this (!) so tells A. to follow his wife's orders, reassuring him that Ishmael will be blessed. Ordained Hagar is given bread and water, exhausted in short order in the wilderness of Beersheba where she abandons Ishmael so death can be a real father to him. What's wrong with these boys saying *our father,* Hagar wonders. Just in time, because Hagar's about to invent the NAACP and the Supreme Court, God reveals to her a well of exceptional water that empowers Ishmael with a dream of becoming one of Egypt's finest, expert with the bow and with his Egyptian wife that Hagar selects, and they all live as well as can be expected ever after in Paran as servants

of the Lord. *These are the descendants of Ishmael…named in the order of their birth: Nebaioth, the first-born of Ishmael; and Kedar, Adbeel, Mibsam, Mishma, Dumah, Massa, Hadad, Tema, Jetur, Naphish, and Kedemah. These are the sons of Ishmael and these are their names, by their villages, and by their encampments, twelve princes according to their tribes… They dwelt from Havilah to Shur, which is opposite Egypt in the direction of Assyria….*

Postscript: As one of his wives, Esau takes a daughter of Ishmael, descendant of a veritable untouchable, Mahalath, his cousin. It is not recorded in Genesis whether or not Mahalath was barren.

Reborn in Morrison's *Song of Solomon,* Hagar who once seduced solemn and solid Abra(ha)m, and was a queen in his house, waited on by his shrinking wife who brought her ex-maid dove's milk after milking their wings, can't even get the Milkman to notice her, his appreciative eyes, hands telling her what deserves love, restoring defiance lost in Egypt, afraid to cross the water, all those hungry days, hungrier sea in the middle of hunger.

CRYSTALS

In 1845 Dr. James Marion Sims had seen it many times,
vesico-vaginal fistula, abnormal passageway
between bladder and vagina through which urine leaks
almost constantly if the fistula is large

as it tends to become after those pregnancies
not quite a year apart in Anarcha and her slave
friends Lucy, Betsey. *If you can just fix this*
the girl said, probably pregnant again, her vulva inflamed,
her thighs caked with urinary salts; from the beginning
he saw his future in those crystals.

Society women sometimes had this too, a remaking of the vulva,
more color, pustules like decorations of which women
were already fond: beads, cultured pearls of pus, status.
Perhaps the design improves in its greater challenge to love
and fondle even in the dark except that there is pain,
inability to hold water.

He tried to help Anarcha first, drawing on what
he was inventing: frontier ingenuity and gynecology,
and operated thirty times, using a pewter teaspoon
that he reshaped, bent and hammered for each surgery,
no sterilant but spit, while she watched; it became
his famous duck-bill speculum too large and sharp
to be respectful, yet it let him look.

Such excoriation, such stretching of the vaginal walls, tunnel
into room; such remembrance of Jericho, prophecy of Berlin
when his mind was to have been on her comfort and healing.

Through the vulva was the way most tried to access her
yet they did not come close. Using

a half-dollar he formed the wire suture that closed
Anarcha's fistula on the thirtieth, it bears repeating, thirtieth
attempt.

For the rest of her life she slept in the Sims position:
on her left side, right knee brought to her chest; she so long,
four years, on his table came to find it comfortable, came to find
no other way to lose herself, relieve her mind,
ignore Sims' rising glory, his bragging in the journals
that he had seen the fistula *as no man had ever seen it before.*
Now they all can.

Anarcha who still does not know anesthesia except
for her willed loss of awareness went on peeing as she'd
always done, just not so frequently and in reduced
volume, hardly enough for a tea cup, but whenever
necessary, the doctor poked, prodded, practiced

then, successful, went gloved and shaven to help ladies
on whom white cloths were draped; divinity
on the table to indulge his tastefulness.

It should be noted
that Anarcha's fistula closed well,
sealed in infection, scarred
thickly

as if his hand remained.

A HOT TIME IN A SMALL TOWN

In this restaurant a plate of bluefish pâté
and matzos begin memorable meals.

The cracker is ridged, seems planked, an old wall
streaked sepia, very nearly black
in Tigrett, Tennessee

where it burned

into a matzo's twin. While waiting
for a Martha's Vineyard salad, I rebuild the church
with crackers, pâté as paste

as a flaming dessert arrives at another table where diners
are ready for a second magnum of champagne; every day
is an anniversary; every minute, a commemoration
so there is no reason to ever be sober

to excuse incendiaries who gave up the bottle,
threw alcohol at the church, spectacular reform

in flames themselves ordinary—there'd been fire in that church
many times, every Sunday and even at the Thursday
choir rehearsals. For years there'd been a fired-up congregation

so seething, neighborhoods they marched through ignited
no matter their intention; just as natural as summer.
There were hot links as active as telephone lines
whose poles mark the countryside as if the nation is helpless
without a crucifix every few yards; pity they are combustible

and that fire itself is holy, that its smoke merges with atmosphere,
that we breathe its residue, that when it is thick and black enough
to believe in, it betrays and chokes us; pity
that it is the vehicle that proves the coming of the Lord,
the establishment of his kingdom, his superiority because
fire that maintains him disfigures us; when we try to embrace
him; we find ourselves out on a limb   burning. The meal

tastes divine, simply divine
and I eat it in the presence of a companion dark as scab,
as if skin burned off was replaced as he healed
with this total-body scab

under which he is pink as a pig, unclean at least
through Malachi.

In my left hand, a dash of Lot's wife; in my right, a mill
to freshly grind the devil; since fire is power
both the supreme good and supreme evil are entitled
to it; most of the time, what did it matter
who was in charge of Job?   Both burnt him.

GLORY

The sun does not really rise; the earth turns and leans
into that perception as it circles a sun busy burning
for the sake of light.

That's what I'd like God to do, burn himself again
for the sake of light. Commit to the bush instead of vacating
when it got too hot, berries burning the hands picking them,
picking Him, Moses suffering heat as they suffer in a Chicago August,
five hundred dropping, no rapture to sustain them, members
of Star of Hope.   There should be more hot etching of stone,
more coal-dark hair burning to gray ash for descent
from Sinai and ego, more wheels to take us for a hot time
in Ezekiel's town of exile along the river Chebar.

There's nothing like burning, the changes it induces,
transformations that are not subtle,   gross advantages
the least of which is light.   The body, always a problem, remade.
This form is ideal for this life and no other.

Fire has taken many before their sacrifice
was understood; most days no one wakes smeared
with ashes of Saint Joan. And most only dream, a vaporous
smoky act, of walking the coals in Suva, neem leaves
on their heads, thoughts cooking, passion igniting.

We know what they were, many of them, not necessarily
their names, but they didn't burn because of name alone that is weaker
than identity, even when name claims it.   Instead
a holy hotness was subverted, furnaces raged
with contention and contagion; putrid ideology reached
a boiling point and sizzled so that it seemed relieving to burn
them all, take their teeth, hair and money, but even burned
they stayed chosen   by faith in something glorious that smoke
became a witness to, lusty and strong;   testimony is fire.   Fire
is alive; needs air, feeds, grows.

Occupied houses sometimes go up in flames; yes, the body is such
a structure.   Sati is such a ritual for widows.   Charring of skin

is not meant to thrill or it would not repulse so many.   But some marvel
at anything bright so intensely do they crave the luminous.

On the whole we are marvelous beings
the way we can adapt and accept such awfulness
as there is everywhere, mixed in, of course,
with what we really want to see: jugglers and safe crossings
on the high wire as narrow as most hope is.

Combustion likewise is marvelous, when the blaze
is spirit ever expanding, enacting some incredible reaching
before firefighters arrive to condemn something
it is a pity to destroy.   There is disappointment
in water mastering glory thought too mighty to be extinguished
but this is not a defect in glory; it is a defect in water.

Now is the ascent of smoke, dark formlessness
suggesting the totality of wretchedness on the horizon
as it spreads and simulates incredibly localized nighttime
focused as are lasers and guilt.

Elijah rode a column of smoke to paradise, and to Oz,
a girl rode one that turned; what was it burned
to make those vehicles?
Women burned for witchcraft, the treason red hot
and only smoke when it was over, wisps, fine and thin
as silk's ambition. Burned for what was probably only
pre-menstrual syndrome or the effects of eating ergot-contaminated
rye bread.   Shadrach, Meshach, and Abednego would
not burn; nor St. Agnes, for whom the fire parted; *whatever water
can do, I can do better,* fire said, content to tickle them.
They missed a chance to be fireworked.

Give yourself to the glory raging
if the moment comes in your lifetime.
Give yourself to the astronomical temperature   where there's
instant outburst into flame, the warmest, the ultimate hospitality.
I don't mean to say embrace it, but if it looks when it detonates
like glory, then take no chances, fellowship

with what little colored boys know
lashed and gasolined on the branches, imperfect crosses
with all the limbs intact, the wood undisciplined, the boys
a wild offering and given to God who could use them
since he's not the God he was in the past when he rejected certain
burnt offerings, clad his favorites in asbestos, outfitted the others
in salt; now he takes whatever he's given, revision into neuter
in the Oxford *inclusive language* new testament
without old biases, without tradition, and without passion.

This much is unchanged: smoke seeks
upward motion and the moment it starts to rise
it's redeemed into atmosphere.   I know
that people are combustible, property of glory.
I tell you there's hope for us
and it's all in our ability to burn.

FIRST GRADE ART:
WHAT MEETS THE EYE

The world full of girls and the sky
a blue-violet band full of vees,
the most emaciated and hungry birds
yet they hover.

As expected: stiff arms and legs,
no joints or musculature

on the girl that is the same
in every drawing, every season,
the life cows crave, and ponies
destined for the carousel.

With a single match, all craving
becomes unconditional burning
as the carousel turns to music
and hosannas, fiery hymns

keeping their promises until
there are embers, ashes
and the cold consequences of faith.

THE LIMITATION OF BEAUTIFUL RECIPES

With the silver ladle that belongs
to both of our families alternating years

we take from under the rose bush
as much dirt as the punch bowl will hold, then add:

talcum, water, Old Spice, Avon's Persian Wood,
Eight O'clock Coffee, cold cream, Comet, Miracle Whip,
pureed clams, salt, lemon juice, and grated pink Camay,
everything on hand in two households except

blessed assurance though we hum as we stir it smooth,
spoon it into Dixie cups, rush to the front yard yelling:

**Cleopatra's Formula without which she was no queen.
Take our word; we're both hundreds of years old, experts
in the business; just look, feast your eyes
on what's yours for 25¢; only 25¢!**

Jimmy is first to let us coat his face, and we aren't ready
to kiss him though I could push Deirdre's mouth on his
as she avoids his eyes. In a week we are rich so we
make a cake and bake Bosco into chocolate bars and

chocolate blotches all over the walls and ceiling, stunned
by the limitation of beautiful recipes.

Even so we take our formula to one of our mothers
who does not notice   the proximity of cure   so busy is she
pulling out her hair. We stare at piles of thin wire

wanting to believe in the freedom and power
dismantling can mean
for a woman who tells us in a voice almost singing

that someone we know is gone, hair, hope, and all.
Taken by bullets to where we are heading, little girls
who defer to wolves and shotguns

in the name of helping our mothers
take the ladle and covered casseroles into the house
where blood dries dark as chocolate, and where morning's

first sounds are wails that become melodic and perfect
as our mothers bow down, the hair of one
tumbling over three shoulders.

—for Deirdre

2
DARK EMBRACE

SECOND GRADE ART: THE STUNNING CHANCES

It could be those terrors more apparent at seven
than at any other time, shadow of needle-nose pliers
meant only to install stereo system, speaker wires
that carry Bach and sweetness
to ears that model one of the shapes of torment
                              but all the forms of grace;   instead

she dares sky and struggle to cross the lines drawn between them. As yet
no blue seeps into the manila void known as demarcation
that refutes the world shifting in her kaleidoscope, lovely but unstable, con-
vulsive, sway and give even in buildings tall as stacked trees, their concrete
roots mingling with bedrock as if they're fundamental

and not monstrosity. The persistence of her brushes scraping nearly
depleted shallow beds of her watercolors gives her the chance to stroke
the canvas of a detached ear that stroking reveals
is a misshapen swan's neck or a whole cygnet contorted for the egg
the way she and everything else are contorted for the world. The chance

to care for the shunned and isolated part as one day she might care for
a breast removed so that it can't kill although there's no longer that hope
of milk, that form of Bach, terror and sweetness as the liquid locates
all the bumpy possibilities of the tongue. She has already

cared for each feather found, some black and successful
from calamus almost all the way to completion, white only at the tip
unlike her father's worried hair. With them, she's made a bird
whose flight she improvises, beginning to understand what

should not be understood—feathers attached to a cast of an ear
whose severance rejects the Bach rising like steam from dew
evaporating into misery when solace again each day becomes vagrant

—only hobos almost kept up with it, and she hardly sees them anymore
or their trains that rust now in their dead stops; she was child in a time that's
now too old to have children, a time whose mechanical fascinations
have had to accept that their turn is over although it seems
there wasn't a chance to play because there wasn't;   instead

there are trips to see the fat world Baby Flo makes, the girl assumes,
by eating, an insatiable hunger to possess sanity, sweetness, solace by eating
up the plagues, tormenting decadence of what tastes so good, it is craved
beyond addiction—her savior after eating all sinful deliciousness
in one awful gulp is too skinny to believe. Daddy rushes her by church

to five hundred warm pounds of woman whose scent is so delicate
it disappears after first notice leaving the girl skeptical for a minute
—which seems to be but probably isn't for the best. Baby Flo's ears
are small as if Baby Flo selects what gets in, only Bach

and occasionally a lesser compliment such as this girl's
nearly believable comment about the brown necklaces
Baby Flo's folds of skin make, the bottom one a brown collar
as proper as Miss Dove's. *Good morning, Miss Baby Flo,*
the girl says, candy lipstick in her hand, dimes in her loafers,
a little tissue in her Lovable trainer

because doubt has managed to prevail

(despite the presence of a woman who really is as big as a temple
the girl has been trying to draw without pen and ink asking questions

that prohibit the seizing of this stunning chance of being lost
not only in Baby Flo's unprecedented opportunity for a heyday of disease
considering the magnitude of the province, but, more importantly, also

in this stunning chance of eternity surrendering
to Baby Flo's undeniable wisdom of flesh).

A WALK THROUGH THE *DARK EMBRACE*

soon leads to the second of *the Five Deaths*
etched and engraved by Stefano della Bella
in which two men carry corpses to be left
as changelings in cradles whose rocking
is not disturbed so efficient is this work. The nearer

skeletal mister with his cargo is a version
of enchanted hedgehog on his rooster, absconding
with a wife to prick all night, one too well bred
to reject him for being a perfect gentleman; not a hand
on her, just judicious use of spines such as in
the manufacture of a crown of thorns.

Medieval naturalists noticed impropriety
in a vineyard the Lord was about to favor
until the hedgehog, favoring it also, shook grapes
from the most productive vine and impaled them
on his spines, providing for a family of heathens.

This mister's legs have no meat; his work does not require
any accumulation of flesh, any deposit of fat.
Good strong bones are all death needs.
Well, sometimes a trumpet.

The woman on his shoulder forms the body
of the bird. They are tangled in such a way
there's no point salvaging their boundaries.
Entwined, the effect is really more ostrich than rooster
and expectations of morning, a crowing, a guttural agony
as betrayal slips out as irrepressibly as a fart.

Her hair, caught in this moment of their running
as if eloping, forms sinewy, lustrous neck, curved
like an affluent avenue revealing statelier
and statelier homes. Her gown feathers, rips

(as do her dreams for she no longer responds
to secular concerns) and surrounds
them both   for death is also carried.   Strange

that death would run with this, nobility
bestowed upon the ostrich by ancients noting
it is the only bird *that has the faculty of urinating,*
a bird mixed up in grace the way it leaves its eggs
on a mound like crucifixion hill for the sun to heat
and hatch, never looking back as it runs towards
a redemption it hasn't questioned, faithful that those
that hatch will also run as soon as they're able, first
softening shells as thick as Good Friday's sepulchral stone
with a coating of honey and personal blood
before taking off from what they parented, as their parents did;
the reverent way of ostriches although they did not come to it
by freewill.   Strange
                              that death clutches this.
It must be the ostrich's speed, up to forty-five miles per hour
in eleven feet strides; there are faster animals
(none are birds), but death is already out of breath
and moves at just that speed himself, not rushing
but not taking his time either.

ξ

Advent

Stefano della Bella has arranged
that one of death's feet be raised.

Toes are barely in touch with ground; any
higher, there'd be canine intrusion, and although

more pee is welcomed by those who know it's holy,
this is ostrich and struthious rapture

about to burst from the biggest possible eggs
that ancients knew contained effluences from

the stars otherwise the vast interior would be wasted
since the chick occupied so little. In Abraham's Ur

Queen Sub-Ad's tomb of the fourth millennium before
this era contained an ostrich egg festooned with lapis lazuli

mounted on a pure gold tripod anticipating Agrippa's lustral
eggs, Ovid's calling of the *old woman who shall bless bed*

and bedchamber, having sulfur and eggs in her trembling hand,
and St. Augustine's dream that put all his hope in an egg

for hope has not reached its goal; likewise the egg is something
but not yet the chicken, not yet the ostrich, not yet the world.

ξ

An end to struthious rapture

Eggs hang
from crucified feet
in a cathedral in Burgos
in Spain.

Inventory of the treasures of Angers:
two ostrich eggs in a reliquary hung on silver
chains
to be placed on the altar of St. René
on Easter, for he too rose from death
at the peak of manhood.

Pliny wrote that he saw a serpent's
remarkable egg of the world, *shape and size*
of a small apple, cartilaginous surface pitted
with holes, very much a polypary, base
of a polyp colony, actually a sea urchin

actually the word made man, body concealed
in shell like the usually understated divinity of Jesus,
spines radiating in all directions like his blessings
and promises from the central pentagonal mouth

proportionally larger than any other mouth
including that of shark; source and proof of power.

There is further proof in della Bella's art.
Ostrich continues on its line, vanishing
in an artistic dot because of perspective;
death and the woman run to their everlasting
humility, a dot, a minute egg, so small
only humility prevails
hatching by faith, as small, into
a second season of vanity to carry away,
to run with, to horde,
pile on the empty plate, a feast
of remembrance.

ξ

The *Garroted Man*

holds a dark metal cross, bitter
sucker. It rises
from his groin.
                    Again maleness is holy
although a cross more properly conjures
the symbol of a woman.

To garrote: tighten an iron collar
around a condemned neck until death occurs
by strangulation or spinal column injury
at the base of the brain. The cross
is optional.

A woman tells me someone
is out to garrote her for her eloquent dismissal
of language she found offensive for its being
inauthentic. She felt the writer was not the one
who'd earned the subject.

José de Goya y Lucientes who etched this punishment
on laid paper had seen it happen in Spain, seen
the instrument of death which can be any instrument
this time the garrote

and this time *garrote* as a name for electronic mail
she claims—for it has not been verified—her computer
keeps delivering: *we will garrote you,* and without benefit
of inflection or sender's legal name, it seems benign
until she's possessed of some spirit to look up that new word

and position herself above what he held steady; penetration,
puncture, death by internal cross; *Oh Jesus,* says the coroner
finally digging it out of flesh not about to surrender
anything else.

—*for S. G.*

ξ

Surrender

Käthe Kollwitz's child run over
in 1910's softground etching begins to split;
she is a series of ribbons, shredded, but aesthetically
appealing the longer you look and see such rending
is the basic structure of everything, the separate bars,
lines and bones, fine on the skirt of the woman hovering
near, for pleats incorporate slits for effect, show
good places to cut or slash; fine of course for the hair
of everyone who brings concern to the scene
but the atmosphere is shredded too
so that rain comes as swords, needles,
refreshing because it is still called rain
and everything believed about rain
is also believed of this massacre.

EASTER

      Dr. Frankenstein feeds his son voltage, juice
fires up the hormones

on the day of unkillable testosterone

      while Mary and Martha heed their spices,
their urges to preserve, not dulled by the impropriety of the kitchen
in which they slaughter lambs and chickens.

HEADS

Along the Chickahominy River in the witness
of grasses, rock-bodied birds, and odor of deer
rising, the Queen of Appomattock brings him water
and he washes the feast off his hands, dries them
with feathers, watches the objectivity of two stones,
two hard and solid heads that speak before Powhatan
of what they know and prove: Fate.

Now to beat out his brains, to clean out an
otherwise fine vessel and put it to use holding
at least praise for those who recognized this potential
long before some others remember in Dallas
to purge the president, to lay in Jackie's lap legacy
no match for any dream:

Jack's head open to raid like a honeycomb.

Maybe Pocahontas is not pure and intends
to taste what first she holds, the nose and ears
as separate from the face as fruits, the hair
growing in such a narrow field it is not wise
to plan an agricultural future.   Exactly what

is on her mind when her head gets in the way
of progress, the perfecting of the slash, clean
and neat, a cutting off of regret?   Is there never
a girl who wants to grow up to be the Queen of Hearts
and openly fond of heads that can be cut as easily
as flowers with the right tools, the ones of Salome

and Lolita?   Salome dances as one would
in a stupor although she is not in one, although
she is as rational as she can be, being Salome.

John's head arrives on a platter, knife
and fork come later, in a civilized moment
when the kiss tastes funny, when she sucks
the lips so white she is sure it is talent, one thing
no one bothers to explain.

TEA BAGS

Remembering, she agitates hand washables
from which dirt streams; delicate things, her white
regulation underwear still damp when she puts it on.

OVERSEEING THE CHERRY

I love them too and was one
of the little girls on swings, ice skates, dresses opening
to display Fruit of the Loom overseeing the cherry, for just a second, the brevity
that proves the truth of the moment and the accident of truth.
It is said
that in a man that is maternal too much has gone awry
to rehabilitate him. That Peter Pan still plays doctor.
That he may be neat, pubic hair combed, tied with a bow.
He may be almost anyone. The accusation will stick anywhere.

Blessed are the pure in heart, the low in spirit
and subjects of the rumors, the co-owners
of the history of deviancy.

It is a form of love, in the same category as what
even popes accept though decline to practice. It happened
in moonlight so kisses were appropriate, good night and good night
again as he tucked youngsters into himself, romantic it seemed
to those spying from afar, aboard spaceships and fantasies.

There is a three-year-old sleeping whose breath floats
in jasmine to my room and leads me to his bedside
where my breath is unrestrained and eager to swallow him
though it is quickly dominated by his nostrils and he is Cupid
in bed and there is no choice except to let him cook my breath
to the consistency of wax even when it falls on him and burns
the easy rest, his arm shadowed on the sheets like a wing until
he moves it waking from dream he does not articulate but that surely
was more wonderful   given the loveliness of his head
than this presence dark and insomniac in the room.

Whatever I am, even the one
who scarcely mothered Jesus, kneeling before him
as shepherdess buying the right for lamb to represent him
and chew the circumcised foreskin, it is no monster
I've brought into the world, but something beyond my genes and proteins,
for they are just alibi; yet if through my tight space, then
humble he is, if not human.

For the pedophile, one kiss
and the gardens and palaces of delight vanish
giving rise to the monster
and others also moon-begotten: werewolf
and vampire heeding the white oracle all night long;
deeply pious and men   underneath their devotion.

AFTER READING *BELOVED*

It's just a question of when,
right after unprotected sex with: strangers,
the boy who loves eternally instantly, a husband,
a husband's friends

or as soon as the first blood appears
on the cotton crotch of the Pam undies
knowing how three drops led to the thought
that led to the birth of Snow White and
the devastation of all her caretakers

or can any time become the right time to control
or revoke a birth as on that episode of *M.A.S.H.*
where the Korean woman swallowed all instinct
to save those on a bus from soldiers trained, like
our soldiers, to overcome reverence?

Need ruined everything; the child screamed
for itself, for its mother, and as soon as it affirmed
its life, the mother's hand clamped tightly against lips
and nose small as a bud.
                                        We know what the atom can do;
Eve pulled down that first red one, split it with her teeth
and survived. We still survive termination, not all of us
but enough to ruin eugenics, politics, sport, and convenience.

Some termination may be necessary to prove this:
The mother on the bus suffocated her baby, refusing
the gas that suspended the consciousness of chickens
because she thought her breast could do it better.
Sometimes it can until well after weaning, and by then,
someone else did it for salvation; Mary did not have to wield
the hammers forcing in nails slightly rounded like her nipples.

IN THE UNHOLY LAND OF SLEEP

All the girls have taps on their shoes
metal crescents like a hard kiss from a mouth
with just one African lip. They walk and
one hears crickets moving towards the church.

There's going to be a six-feet tall chocolate bunny
for children to whack at after giving their rhyming
speeches. Everything that comes out of their mouths
must be music. Even this brief death

that is the reason for the rabbit. With such ease
young girls almost click their heels and speak of
rising as if that stunt compensates for the horror

of the scourging, the piercing of his sides, the vinegar
in the sponge, not to mention the blunt edges of old Roman
nails that despise skin, rip skin, splinter bone. The vine
of blood that wound down the base of the cross. He rises

quickly, a stunt that does not compensate for the challenge
of being buried under the tonnage of all the sin ever
to be in the world.   After this
there are demands for ears, and the tail

round as a world; hands and faces take home
chocolate success and switch to movies about vampires
and zombies who don't respect the grave either, who
after leaving it behave strangely, a stare and lock-kneed walk,
a reconfiguration into bat or divinity who floats and fades
like the narrow contrail of a jet.

A MAN

How handsome he was, that man who did not court
the girls fawning all over him as if he'd already saved them,
it's my leg, one said, raising her hem as she'd raised it in dreams
he knew of, for everything reached him as prayer, *my leg, Sir,*
is not perfect although as he looked, it glistened and the blood
became more productive. He did not date, nor rendezvous in tunnels and tents,
did not kiss except to heal, did not harass, malign nor mutilate;
threw no stones

       and he was a man; never forget that he was a man,

that being a man improved him. Before the mothering, He was a solo act
ramming omnipotence down the throats of Ramses, Job, all the sinning nobodies
of Sodom. He was feared before he was born a triplet of flesh completing
the one vaporous, the other heavy and strict; now he's desirable, vulnerable;
in the mother he visited stages of: fig, fish, pig, chicken, chimp before settling irrevocably
on a form more able to strive. This was a more significant time in darkness,
gestation of forty weeks, than three days in a hillside morgue; he learned maternal heartbeat
and circulation of her blood so well they became dependency,
and so he learned that some radiance is not his, hers

came in large part just from being Mary—how content she was even before pregnancy,
betrothed, blushing to ripen the fields; content even before she knew of angels,
and now, with this mound of baby, she was parent of a world whose prospering
she encouraged, activity of fish, magma, sulfur, the earth striving
      just as she did.

He was a man
         yet the usher of miracles, preaching on a mountain
where reverberation gave him the power of five thousand tongues, yet not
a big man, not athletic, ordinary looking except for that glow and doves circling
him in the desert, doves that had been vultures earning their transfiguration
by consuming decaying meat just as he ate all the sin; for that flattery, he bid them dip their
feathers in his eye, drawing into them that sweet milk around the iris.

He was a man
         when he began to understand love, erasing the lines between
Gentile, Jew, and invited any who wanted to come to his father's house for bottomless milk,
honey, ripe fruit, baskets of warm bread and eggs, wine, live angels singing. Weary revelers

could lay their heads on his breast, he said, needing intimacy; he thinks
as a man, therefore

$$he\ is\ a\ man$$

and good times, memories can be
adequate heaven. He knows the distance a man
is from his father, how likely it increases till the deathbed; he knows

what a man knows

the now and here, and can be called by name,
and can be wounded, and must struggle, and must be proud
every now and then or could not continue, must be worth something,
must be precious to himself and preferably to at least one other, must be,
in these thousands of post-Neandertal years, improving, must have
more potential, becoming not only more like God, but more like
what God needs to become, so moves also,
so God moves also

because a man moves.

DECISION

Really Lazarus decided himself that he didn't like the tomb;
death left little to his imagination; mostly he was numb
and having to concentrate tremendously just to believe
in toes, shins, but he was adamant about it, missing color his dead eyes
failed to interpret being unable to commute the stay
of darkness. He did not relent until the bones trembled

so vigorously with decision that the Lord perceived movement
that opposed His own. Defiance is not necessarily unattractive, on that day
was welcome diversion; mist had situated itself in valleys and was a thin layer
of peace, a weak hymen that no one, save Lazarus, rushed to violate.
Impressed, the Lord called him, granted permission for rebellion

that for a minute stopped as Lazarus reconsidered
just whether or not the need had really been his own;
his decision was weakened by the call and by death's apparent rejection of him;
wasn't he good enough for darkness in which he was beggar, totally dependent
on dark congress?
Just what did he own in the chamber that was somewhat reticent
about wanting him, not pushing toward him
as he pushed it away? Had death been holding its breath, hoping
this man would get the hint and leave as quietly and quickly
as he had arrived, so that death could feel freer without this inadequate
presence that refused to melt and relinquish authority, that populated
the cavern with thoughts drifting like mermaids and all their vanity
and temptation? Convinced he could not die well

Lazarus went about the departure wondering how he could explain
the lack of loveliness when only he was there, the lack of fire
when he was sure that same heart was helping him now to rise and take steps
to prove that this is truly an hospitable world whose fruits are for him,
whose textures are for his pleasure, and who does not mind that he invents
the language of mastery, that he aspires, challenges, does not notice the tomb shrink
like a post-partum uterus, that the difficulty of its accommodating him was all
in his mind that itself entombs myriad good ideas he has wasted
to conclude that he's on top of the world.
                                        He must step lightly
on this road he travels renewed, confident, repressing the truth
that he brings to death nothing new.   One hard step and he'll sink

for there are pockets in the earth, envelopes; untrustworthy patches
into which he could slip, and rescue may not repeat; willpower
is unreliable, this lean determination will grow flabby and next time
won't have the strength of mind over matter; the matter of his body
will acquire a heaviness active tissue lacks, an immobility and fixed stance
a living mind resists, changing and fickle in its causes and beliefs,
and the Lord, who truly loves this man, may not call him again

no matter that Lazarus becomes the ultimate supplicant, that his prayers
moist with nether weather are so poignant they remain in the sky, additional
bright celestial hopelessnesses to inspire though they merely reflect and do not
generate their light; no matter, for the radiance is but a promise,
and some dates and loves, even first loves, don't call you anymore, leave you
high and dry, and there you are, alone with your broken body begging: here, take,
eat, consume, digest, and I'll be your little bit of excrement, devoted little bit of shit.

THE SAINT AND THE MODERN EQUIVALENT
OF THE MIRACLE OF LACTATION

Like others, he resists women
though not easily, Benedict rolls naked in thorns, Bernard
throws himself into frigid water that steams around him, a curtain
a hooker parts to get in bed with him, but he cries *robbers, thieves!*
and she flees without the replacement chastity she wanted. He knows the ways
of women so well
he will not, once he has such power, admit Humbeline, his sister,
to the convent, but she retaliates and does not ever consummate her
marriage, is not even tempted to, gets in that way. Though Aleth, his mother,

had her pick of wet nurses, she wanted her six sons, seventh daughter to have
only her noble milk, mother of six monks, a seventh nun. But despite these efforts,
even her children made waste. The body is the point of contact

with sin; every detour from redemption is made by the body; Bernard
flees the world so that it can not touch him, desirable son of a knight. First
he's Bernard of the Valley of Wormwood, green in the Cistercian Order
trying to overcome the senses that cause one to fall in love
with things seen, heard, smelled, touched, tasted—none of which is involved
in loving God. He resists sleep
so as not to snore obscenely, a carnal call he did not want to master,
                    And he's offended
when the Abbot is impressed, sending him deeper in the wilderness
to build a house at Clairvaux where he repents all his life
with a loyal diet of boiled beech leaves that promote him to *Doctor Mellifluus,*
the honey-sweet abbot, monks chasing his stern skirt for more deprivation,
that dreadful, home-cooked barley bread, like that which Aleth made
with her own milk that did not dry up so that her breasts retained virtue,
maternal status.

Clairvaux means radiant like fame.
130 monks heed the beacon. Consider how a miracle

must be pursued by accident; Bernard intends only to repent with his diligence
and denial; consider
that it is not during his first sitting with the icon
that it happens, despite alabaster's milky prediction. His meal

is only prayer at the feet of a virgin, kiss of the stone foot
pale as if all blood has been lost, cloudy as if still burdened.
He can not give birth to anything and is sorry at his fallen
lot to receive those graces he can't stop well after
he's had more than his share.   Mary the tower
humbling him each night.   He's sorry

and keeps at those feet of the statue that is one artful
long bone. Each time he sees a new aspect
of her holiness; before her, his knees protrude
from his surplice like breasts that dig into Mary's mercy, the soft part
of stone that persuade her to give him *The Miracle of Lactation* when
he prays, *Monstra te esse matrem,* for it; for him she expresses milk
that arcs to Bernard's lips. He prays to know whether to lick
or let it dry.   After

sexual reassignment surgery, the modern equivalent happens centuries later
to a man who for God abandons his old life, submits to knife
wielded by an anointed in medical habit, surgical gown and mask, treating
a supplicant as if he'd been an unrehabilitatable rapist; the patient is cut
and stitched just as, before needing to become one, he'd seen a woman
cut and stitch poultry, plug it with sage, rosemary; he wants himself stuffed
with myrrh where now he is open to common assault. Even

as he sleeps, his breasts develop, sprouting
from what was always within him. Only this way
can he give to God what he really wants God to have
(perhaps what God really wants; everything is in His hands
and some of those things, He strokes).   Like the saint, he prays for milk
he can force through a bite from his partner's blessing teeth; it hurts
as it should, becoming a woman although he was born a black sheep.
Those costly silk purses he made from sows ears sit next to ash trays
made from silverback hands, but it's still good to see someone
taking chances on craftsmanship, on making things, since usefulness,
even of faith, has not been weaned from luck.

LINES FOR A WET NURSE

She slips in the back door
using silence for key
moonlight for milk.

SAINT ANTHONY'S ECSTASY

To the poor, Anthony gave everything so none went lacking
at his expense. His own resulting poverty did not count
since it was accomplishment.

A seductress once joined him in bed thinking he was alone
although God had a stake in the sheets. Seeing his ecstasy

when the only contact executed was her smell tangled
in his breathing of necessity, she mistook God again

as her chance, so there burst from her bodice indisputable harvest
when she undid one blue ribbon
in the nick of time revealing a brown stain on each tip

of milk loaf, the mark of the devil's mouth,
defiled bread, devil's food, and he refused to set his lips
to any body but the body of Christ.

As these loaves fused and combusted, the demon fornication
appeared in that harsh hospitality as the black child
he really was, no lady, nothing that could possibly tempt

Anthony who announced that seeing such ugliness
killed all his fear

just as it killed the fear of some men in the Memphis
this Anthony didn't know, men who seeing black girls
bought them and having paid knew what to do to them:

A crop of children half demon, half success like the race
of centaurs, manticores, bishop-fish, mermaids

still known as Other
though not the other of the Golden Rule. Anthony's

black boy retaliates, calls upon his buddies: Nat Turner, Toussaint,
other homies who butcher Anthony's flesh thinking to annihilate
but flesh had been Anthony's only weakness

and for its destruction, he loved God more for allowing his perfecting
and God loved his interpretation, the confounding brightness

originating in Anthony's mind and spilling into his cave in the wilderness.
Bread, only coarse bread eaten severely with minimum salt and water
to force it down   every three or four days   brought to his

ruins high above the Nile every six months by the only man Anthony
theoretically could see twice a year but the deliverer knew where
to leave the bread, the stone that camouflaged it, the accident

of Anthony kneeling, praying and finding the miracle of food
then being too ecstatic to eat.

SPLITTING A DOUBLE LIFE

As if having the best of everything isn't going to rob her of too much,
dull her doubt that has been the source of all her energy; she coaxes
this man, preferring that to messing up her own initiative, to exceed
his destiny and split himself as neatly as she has severed the best
from the mediocre when in accepting his proposal, he had to accept hers.

In the worst of all places where anyone is most vulnerable, in front
of a mirror that has been lied to, she tells him the double vision
of standing there proves it can be done; he is already split from himself,

the reflection has its own mind and heart that are flat and base, uncaring,
unaffected by the senses that are part of the three-dimensional habit
of indirectness. She's his wife now and even more romantically

greedy for his selves, their differences. He's a physician, already
used to splitting his time between her and other women
who must mean nothing   though they are naked the first time
he sees them; they draw, as he approaches, the draped sheet
from modesty to a tight fit, the opposite from what they intend

yet he must not respond to innocence as he'd like, to indulge it,
celebrate it as a free man would when he becomes one in
a courtroom. *You can do it,* she says as if he battled paralysis in a leg
and needed to walk to the bathroom instead of battling man's nature.

The formula does not look or smell compelling, any old drink
though fate is in the flask, and he's suspicious of the ability
to separate good from evil, to rank as gods or devils; he can not believe
even if he succeeds in the new tradition of Dolly, the ewe he loves, in giving birth
to himself as twins—what *born again* has alluded to all along. After this
all will queue as for the Salk oral vaccine and drink it
or if uncooperative receive it injected as they will also, that same day, receive
Christ's blood—he sees a glorious future—saved whether or not they want salvation,
all of us born again and again. God, *glug, glug,* how he loves her

and how he wishes he hadn't seen so many bad Jeckyll and Hyde movies
bent on dark constructions as monstrosities and brutes, physical differences.
He will know the subtle constituents of good and evil and then each may be cooked up
in the laboratory according to need. He assumes despite the physiological sameness

that it will be obvious which is which
and that his wife will know the distinct psychology embedded in their hearts
and lift herself from polyandry, perhaps letting the more skilled of the twin doctors
split her, one for each, matched or unmatched sets, depending on the more
promising chemistry. Splitting all that a man is must be easier, he hopes,

than the task of the Manhattan Project. He wants most to eradicate
the blending and fading into the poles of the spectrum that creates conscience,
questions, indecisiveness. To know the authenticity of evil and then easily
destroy it will spare us mistakes, bring that elusive image in which we were made
into focus. Mercy is the child of doubt from which his work will free first himself
and then the rest of us. Certainty is his objective.

But the body; what a problem, for he can not perform such surgery
on anyone let alone himself—the clone is another infant, and he wants
an immediate secondary adult to house all his baseness. His spirit
will be divided swift and true, each part weaned from the other in simple
cranial manipulation, all foul perception shifted to one hemisphere, than split
down the middle, like rump or peach, but his heart will not double, liver, penis,
tongue, head; only certain anatomy is conveniently in pairs and sets, the problem
of those born conjoined forcing physicians to sometimes choose who gets
the body. Still, his work will help them choose better until we learn
to take advantage of corpses we stop revering, until we can construct
from some wonder polymer, houses for halved spirits. To split into instant
full-grown replica is his mission. However, once separated,
might he not recognize evil

                    as his vitality and inspiration?
Goodness prefers passive resistance, trusts inertia, calls it *patience* and *virtue*.
His wife wants a bad boy to make love to her, one of the seven virile angels
of the Apocalypse, one of whom Desdemona thought she had in Othello.
We don't ever see it scientifically isolated to know that evil is as bad as it seems
while it must continuously fight goodness, while both try to occupy the same space
How will it behave when the war is over?
                    That is all the good doctor wants to know.

71

ODE TO THE CAT-HEADED CONSORT
IN A PAINTING BY BOSCH

Demons loved Anthony; he could go nowhere, do nothing
without demonic entourage, demonic interpretation; every footstep
threatened to release from hell a spirit where the earth cracked
under the weight of Anthony's walking judgment. Pure

physical attraction, the white hot whore masturbating in a hollow tree,
her right hand like unto bark, the tree could not resist her, *am I now to be damned*
by the woods where I sought to lose the world? Barren tree of the fallen Eden
whose opening is like the labia majora of a giantess, the only shelter in a storm
so Anthony begs God to cauterize him with an electrifying heavenly burst
that incinerates all evidence of balls and phallus that swells with sin, the disease
for which there is no cure, just mercy; that increases most vilely in the night
for which he has prepared by fasting, reciting scripture, binding his genitals tight
with prayer cloth and twine, but dawn brings with it priapism, indictment
and commitment

to manhood that holds and reduces him; it was this instrument that defeated Adam
in his sleep—hear now, Boys, the truth of Pinochio—and wound around
the tree like a miracle, according to Eve who saw it move and flex, stay alive
while the rest of Adam died in sleep. *Damn*

the thing, fat with pride, rigid as sword and swift punishment, the Devil's tail,
the center and most important tine of his three-tined pitchfork. Seek
a doctor? Submit to touch, inadvertent pleasure? Here is mine
own rod with which to tame the beast of itself; fully prepared

to mate, not to meet the Lord with this libidinous snake of Medusa's pubic
hair, a hardness like the heart of Pharaoh. The harlot stands in water
too murky to consecrate, the only water in which immersion won't redeem
for it is too full of desire whose diaphanous crystallizing filaments reach up
from the pool to her thighs and hindquarters, extending from there to a gluttonous devil
whose head rests in a devilish horned flower, whose right hand holds a bowl
into which flows iniquity from a chalice that does not pour, but seems to bleed
its liquid. The canopy is red although advent is white, red for these profane nuptials
in which sin couples with everything. The whore white as perfection's aspiration

is of swollen belly for in her sin incubates, and her cat-headed consort catches for her
a fish ruined for having to depend on water she controls; why, semen evacuates its gills and
travels the thin tubing of the web, the snare to enter her where she guides it. Fish
and whore carry a like number of eggs, odors.

There is one watching her, enjoying her unaware she knows his gaze and whispers of it
to the consort. The watcher can see but her hand, but it grips the bark tantalizingly
and he feels the pulsing travel the wood to his hand that grips a darker element
of the same tree.

    It doesn't look like it, but the bird perched is some sort of partridge
for those are the fowl most prone to inelegance, *frequent intercourse tires them out*
and the male defeated in fights for a mate *submits to venery like a female.* It is not
the woodpecker it seems, but disguised just as the man in gracious turquoise
dispensing communion to one it intoxicates, one too far gone in sin to be resuscitated,
is neither angelic nor ascetic, naked under the robe for the convenience of the whore
whose bounty of red gown lavished over the dead tree would, wrapped around her,
suggest indefatigable modesty; one who would ravish her would be discouraged
by the miles of cloth though the red encourages diligence, but she is not wearing it
as Anthony keeps to his scriptures—he shall not want her.

He'd wanted to be a good man, but it is best not to be a man at all
for men become their constituents; as embryos, men are fed a progression
of beastly status so that if one is born prematurely, he can't be called man
but must be regarded as the station in which he stops, swine, for instance, or salamander.
Circe guided men to their roots. This is why men can't ever be any better
than they are right now. This is why they are no better than pigs, dogs, the lowly
animals men are, on their way to becoming men, and this is also why
there is any chance at all for humility.

3

LUMINOUS LYMPH

TWO THINGS

Before going any further I must ask that two things
be taken into consideration

although *consideration* is too mild; most raises solicited
have disappeared in consideration

But these two things nevertheless exert some measure

changing what otherwise would be, these two

just two things

the one that this city has soft water; those who do not
depend on wells have flowing in their pipes soft water

that is also what is boiled for steam in even the most archaic
radiators of choice or circumstance.

Soft water is a big deal for in it skin and laundry become
more clean with less effort and soap rinses off more

thoroughly but mostly, it's just that word *soft*
that appeals to linemen, factory workers, foot soldiers

as well as to those expected, for all these love so like,
at least occasionally, to rub against softness

that sometimes, face it, is unbelievable.

Free of mineral salts, my taps run free of mineral salt

nevertheless there is a water softening system
in my basement—the previous lady of the house,

and including me
there's been just two,

had skin especially fine, practically colorless although
she did not consider herself worthy of albino classification

—*I am not even that*
she says, lingering in the house, vaporous

the way her life was   even with bodily presence demanding endless
refining, distilling, reducing to air, her residue hoping

that with it I will make soft-water tea

(and say this salt prayer)

We soften what is soft, chastise what is already chastised
just by being born

and have fifty-pound bags of salt, three left,
that perform this unnecessary act of sending

each night into the sump pump
hundreds of gallons of salt water as our soft water tries

to become softer, tries for superlative certain
to be outdone, the Guinness records automatically obsolete

as is everything else; no way to keep up
to commit to accuracy, the purity that is accuracy

and the sump pump fails.
The salt

has corroded it. It fails.

Water backs up, disobeys pipes there
to lead it to a promised freedom, freedom

is always the promise, even when truth makes it,
setting free the water

that is free just long enough to be trapped
in padding under the carpet

reviving mummified Play-doh

and anointing wood, three walls of book shelves
and the books on the bottom.

We've had a flood, that is how the insurance company
handles it, as flood as true as something in the Dakotas

and Minnesota: Flood.

—Even when we seem to, we don't speak the same language
for each tongue, each brain means something slightly different

and something slightly different from what is actually spoken

and written.

But two things—well, this too is promise
as is everything

but for now, just the other thing,

that my home was built for a family unfamiliar
with American culture and proud, very proud of that—their first

corporate assignment in the states—

she, the former lady, whispers as if the gesture makes her
prouder, but pride is big enough—can't get bigger—so it's squandered

and everything spawns it so that there is not enough shame
not anymore.   In the absence of the American dream

although arguably any house at all fulfills it

but in the absence, the house tends towards modesty, held back
only by that pride

that honestly, not wanting to lie to me so much, she whispers that she
enjoys, former lady

who also would have enjoyed what her choices at the time denied:
glass doors that would slide into suburban deck and offer constant

view of the Charmglow.   My house

is without living room and formal demands
usually made without regard to either personality

or inadequacy.   Solidly middle-class house

knowing better than to pretend to be more, held
in check by that small lawn a quality picnic blanket
would completely conceal

so I do not find myself without need
to apologize

—so many expect and need for what they think I am and have
to have a legitimate claim to opulence

beyond ability to say the words *legitimate claim to opulence*
yet I could lie

and years later apologize for that
although, thanks to the lady's example, I enjoy

the way a lie unravels to again a single, flexible thread

that really could have been true

so I do prefer truth, what should be truth

what is truth, that after all, it remains
my fate, my condition to be ordinary

though fiercely I've resisted that truth above all truth

as if shame must follow the mundane, the mundane
that is what all ritual must become

the repetitions of *I love you* no matter what percentage of them
is true for I've said it to a plate of spaghetti

promptly consumed for offering the tastefulness of lies fully unbound

dissolution of the maze so no more sense of coming out of darkness.

At first I'm disappointed to be no different from anyone else
although I can't prove that I'm not

and then glad again for words like *brotherhood*
that won me a fifth grade prize in poetry

although the word and what I realized for it were common,
ordinary, just as what always inspires us, water stain (iridescent in light

       so simply mother of pearl)

on the glassy exterior of an office building in Clearwater, Florida
becomes the latest appearance of the Virgin, the lady

purposely mundane in my house in order to be believed

and yet this culture, that building, this house, all structures, ideologies
—like the dismantled softening system—deteriorate, fall, burn, recede

or are washed away

by water soft sometimes, sometimes salty

and oh so true

are the shrines,   thousands of shrines the water leaves behind.

THOSE IMMORTAL AXILLARY ANIMALS

Bagpipes when the fragile animal is squeezed
produce sounds of a lamb before it has seen or heard
another lamb and so bleats without influence
when squeezed by someone seeing it a first time, blocking
thoughts of braised mutton with the delight of that first viewing.

Someone afraid both not to squeeze and to squeeze
something physical out of the spiritual. Then there come
paresthesias that almost paralyze so exciting are the prickling
and itching as he nearly resists an irresistible urge to play those animals.

Then comes awareness of unspeakable delights
that come only when the axillary animals are held close
to the lymph where they are like another filter, another line
of defense, the new lamb sounds luring infection and pus
into the bag the musician squeezes and relaxes as if truly
he's massaging the very last chance, trying to be clinical about it
and failing, rubbing the heart even the delectable one
of calf or pig, touching what is so like the part of himself
he can not touch, surgeon or musician, priest;
                                        whatever he is
his fingers lengthen and rely on lessons of air touching
the untouchable and surviving, blowing and whistling itself
into a tight swirl of fetal pleasure, designed, like everything
except the animal itself whose permanent job is to inspire, to be temporary
so as to never quite extinguish longing.

He squeezes and cries a cry the animal respects, allowing its sound
to disappear in his, only to then swallow his, for the animal's sound
is bigger and the disappearance was strategy, the man virgin no more
in subsequent dealings with the animal,
                                but let him play it whatever his maturing
motives; let man earn respect and forgiveness by endearing himself monogamously
to this animal that sings after thousands of squeezings as if there's no need for ambition
to exist, and let him need each time to hear the song, not to sing it
or even to write it; let him be amazed that he can touch the animal
in a way that makes it sing like this; let him realize that it could

have been years ago that he touched his animal, years ago that it sang him
to sleep and eternity and saved him the trouble of wakefulness
in which his senses get involved in logic and discipline
instead of in the unconscious discoveries of slipping away, going under,
being dazzled in a coma as feminine as his first encounter: his mother's
soft gown moving as if acquiescing to water as it opens

to reveal a soft tan animal his mother presents to his mouth
and squeezes as he sucks, an animal her hand cups like a brain
holding every solution, miraculously free of disease considering
how perfectly human it is, white as coral—oh hasn't this been every dream,
the sight of the brain as what titillates the fragile animal in our heads?—Peter
the Great gazing at the jars of brains in his collection, his eye enlarging
in the distortion of red fluid, glass, and light.

KING KONG

Into a ballroom that big hand
extends. All the bare-back women have magnetic
skin—bingo! chorus line in his palm

and when he snaps his fingers: dervishes
dominoes, Vesuvius.

MACAQUES CHECKING EACH OTHER
FOR LICE: A PUBLIC DISPLAY

Finding lice, they pop the grubs into their mouths
and wrap them in saliva, *fold them in* according
to recipes; picture the dipping of truffle particles

into Belgian chocolate—mere monkeys
if they were able to shake their elegance
in this dirty game. Now *this* is the way

to eat Raisinets in the theater.

Look at the one brushing back hair
with the left hand while the right hand snatches
a nit as if a kiss has been stolen, the head angled

as if to whisper in the ear thanks for the red face being
so honest it is right for a bowl of delicacy, rare
night bloom superbly lit, a blush

is an exemplary flower.

Noticing a wooden piggy's slashed back,
a macaque reaches and soothes
causing coins to fall from between her fingers, soft

and molten, as if she's scooped out a volcano
to use the heat of earth's oldest neighborhood
to tame her mate's hair, the burn of magma

and konk   burning like vision, madness, fervor
in a groupie of the saints who would climb Macchu
Picchu, hoping to be a bird or something

with the kind of soul so perfect it need not have will,
its flight serving just to create descent
to the healing stream to spawn the angels and die. At

the summit there is an artichoke unlike any other
for life is only a matter of altitude, not taste.
Macaques are in charge

of the peak artichoke, peering into its petals
as if checking for nits tucked in; why, it's the artichoke
of the ear! the incomplete human flower!

Thank macaques
for this potential.

CHEATING

The cheating belongs to a season that can not be resurrected.
And each spring has memory so is not original. I know only
of how it was for Lazarus and that account from a man
who had no real cheating to explain.   Cheating death
is honorable.

When Lazarus left his tomb the way I left the house that day,
entirely too casual for what was happening, he did not bring with him
a trail of bees and flowers to show the depth of summer; he did not
shiver the chill of transition, rays of light crinkling
behind him to suggest the imminence of snow somewhere
in the world. The season of Lazarus
is unknown and gone.
                                He was called, but was not called again;
he died at least twice and knew injustice, believed the first—and last
it turned out—calling was a promise; in faith, he was willing
to die endlessly, to enter into contract and die just so the caller
could call and become known for calling, but the dependency
was not balanced; Lazarus did all the needing, the caller, all
the cheating, unless, of course, the caller be called God; that
name-calling changes the picture; lucky Lazarus, alive
to fear God again.

But that is too big to really matter; most of living is
small and unimportant, uninspiring. In this case, for instance,
it was a musician's way of asserting that I was the only woman
in the world though we sat in a cafeteria, the deep fat smelling tooled
and seductive, pointing to seams in the cow girled server's hose
as platters came close to our noses.   Then
he brushed strands of hair away from my eyes
as if brushing away bits of eraser
after making the picture of me perfect.

This isn't the time to wonder just what it was
I did for him in 1975, a season gone and increasingly
insignificant; we came together as any strangers can.
What allows some strangers to go past strangeness, exchanging
what is called depth although no depth of human understanding
or intelligence has been indisputably proven? Mostly it is as if

I don't care about the world, for most of its population
consists of strangers; it is as if I welcome their losses for fulfilling
the day's quota of loss so that my day may be sweet and frivolous,
but the musician and I did more; we allowed vulnerable connections,
spoke of dreams about to evaporate unless we breathed life
on them for each other, as if spousal breath would be inadequate
in its familiarity, as if I knew a husband could no longer console who had
once cheated on me because he didn't really know me or himself or
the limitations of living, the truth of human inadequacy

that we accept the way finally we accept our age, and understand that coupling
is entirely choice, not mandate; that in chemistry, any atoms of hydrogen
and oxygen will partner into water, that widows survive and still
have moments of happiness; reproduction isn't even necessary, the world
is not only for our species or necessarily for any species at all, the dead Jupiter
and Neptune go on rotating and revolving without audience or chronicler; Earth
can survive without us; our purpose is not maintenance of the world
but of ourselves.   Any two

can wed or cohabit; we choose to be faithful, to cut ourselves off
from all other sources of pleasure and fulfillment, for life in its variety and profusion
assures that multiple compatibility is possible; we choose not to look for
the other perfect matches, the one in each million; we choose. My husband

is my Lazarus; I call him from the tomb where misery is everything.
It is all about suffering; that is what people do, suffer the trivialities
we have called important because they are ours and are all that we have,
among them our movies and investments, as if value is something other
than our own delusion; we are not

what has become of the pioneers and dreamers; they are dead and they
had no knowledge that could predict the likes of the world now; it
is a place they would not recognize, perhaps would not be able to cherish
although as its antecedents, they might try to claim credit, might want to believe
that they are somehow responsible for our progress, such as it is. These

lies do not cheat the truth; the truth is ever present and known,
but it is truth and therefore is undesirable in its immutability.
The truth is finished; it is not lovely architecture and is self-made
and is also the only originality, not expandable nor reducible
and really doesn't affect our lives, existing independently

and somewhere else, not in the board, court or class rooms, but nearby
and untouchable; our cheating does not disrupt it. Truth

actually has very little to do with life since it seems
to be the point of the grave, but if that is all that truth is, it is not
particularly useful; it is then too accessible to be useful.

SOUR MILK

*It doesn't matter to me if the cow comes from the left,
the middle, or the right side of the pasture; I'm concerned
with whether or not the milk is sour.*

—*Stanley Crouch*

At first

Sour milk poured same as good milk from
the glass pitcher slim and smooth as dreams
required of women

then clumps, knots, smelly coagulating rosary; no,
make that little Adam's apples tumbling
into drain, disposal to help them degrade

on the night ice is believed to drift on Europa's watery pact,
on the night that Cleveland babies hemorrhage, lungs touched
by spores and cells of sooty-looking mold, stachybotrys bacteria
thriving on dampness, leaks,

poor drips

in east side basements, visiting water and air, hello
signs of life, parasitic truth and rubric of all life living off
other life, that urge turning out to be mold, spoiled

by a lack of divinity.   Then

came the question, the suspicion
of souring occurring upon human contact—it
wouldn't be the first time such contact upset

a balance, wracked out an ecosystem although
our very lives depended upon just such errant
fortune, the deluge, the extirpation of dinosaurs

against whom our spines would prove no challenge
despite spine's purpose, a certain souring
of perception.   Of course

souring, spoilage happen when milk exceeds
its shelf life, when mishandled, kept warm
as compassion; when it has resisted

pasteurization or when it's just born bad—as
when it has suffered through an ulcerating perforation
instead of evacuating udders, for primordial life incubates

in milk and needs just a chance to proliferate, in total
devotion to survival, a devotion our brains
do not learn as well, for in their excess capacity,

we learn other lessons simultaneously
so the extras, the incidentals
seem just as important.   What

if milk sours in the cow or in the goat?—more easily believed
perhaps because of the goat's status or the pig's, milk
defiled by definition, soured in the nanny goat and sow, the swill
of swine, of mother
to swine; attitude expressed

so that the father too can feed the scions.   I'm thinking

about what I've been fed tonight: Galileo spotting signs of Jovian
moon life, the bleeding bursting through infantile lungs where
I grew up, the east side, when the offending pipes were good
as new, the plaster perfect, or seems so now while the present sours
and the direction of wholesomeness begs to be the past despite
what else is there: all that life we couldn't see

in the wallflowers, the geeks, the doofus the homecoming queen
married in the only madness her prettiness allows, all that life aborted
—not that no one is helped by this, more perhaps than helped

by that life of Riley

and all the microbes it spawned, that feasted
on Riley's sloughed cells, the mites under his bed in the dust, ducts
—fungal roses, toe jam, life neglected but life to treat like life, to save

from the next flood of intolerance.

Milky roads and whatever
paradise can be

in bovine hemorrhage

of what is

                    Sour
                    in the cow.

Heifer, Cow

are what the family of the victim called the woman
who was a victim of her country, her company—dominoes—her body's
susceptibility to life, three pregnancies she was aware of, but not

the multiple births within her, pathological births
of viruses within her, souring her vaginal secretions so that
they washed his penetration with infection (of which pleasure

may be a form), microbes, toxic flags announcing take-over, pirating
of the 5'7" country of my brother-in-law, gonorrhea, herpes both deposed
by HIV, imperial sickness, his body the royal conveyance

as he sleeps counting trips he made to Mexico (birth of his freedom,
toasts to Pancho Villa, Fritos—he was so crazy, in love with life)
everything sounding better in Spanish, his rejections, his name

that he changed while he was there, itinerary in hand, beginning
with a search for a woman *(la vaca)* who knew all the tricks of corn
that he knew in Muncie, every summer working the fields, putting

in his pockets something that hadn't been in them before, novelty
like the first months of his disease. South of the border

he has his face painted on black velvet, a softness
none of us remember.

     Pero, hijos, hijas, we do recall

those long trips to places someone will call home,
for life is everywhere, in extreme heat, extreme cold;
some form of life traveling in our suitcases, on our tongues

as we sleep in Cougars and Opels, as we recall caterpillars
with hair like Beethoven falling from trees, dripping, leaking.
Full of the spirit, branches swayed and jerked in storms as if

they'd leaned against the sanctified church all their years, not
his window. *All the cattle are standing like statues, but a little*
brown maverick is winking her eye, knowing it's

Sour in the cow.   She loved him, she loved
him not, loved him   on a pallet on the floor, comfortable
until his i.v. got in the way of the rectangle on the floor, his
panel in the miles and miles of quilt, the distance

love is supposed to last.

And God, don't forget that God loved him
and loved P. T. Barnum—has to love a good hoax,
a literality in which His being love

unifies all theories   :)

Likewise, I am sugar and spice married to snakes and snails
and both of us just as edible as lion, king (sounds good, but it's
not the highest rank despite what some have assumed about the lion

life) of beasts, served in La Jolla for a hundred dollars a plate, Top
of the Cove where I ate John Dory for much less—some first tastes
are heavenly, out of this world   as was

the *Venus Hottentot* and every negrified woman raised to oddity, stretched
necks, lips, ears able to bear saucers, lobes birds could fly through, entire
continents were dismissed as circuses. We can mutilate ideas, the body, or genetics

can produce hirsute faces, dark and lycanthropic until years turn hairiness gray,
white; we are all purified by old age, even the lifers, the criminal elements
denied the periodic table and the rest of education that may have kept them straight

or at least more likely to commit white collar, sour milk crimes
the monkey girl, alligator boy are more willing to excuse, knowing
as the scripts of talk shows remind us, that freaks can never be appreciated

in quite that way again—*it's the nineties*—according to embarrassing and
indignifying anthropological recipes, use the indicated (all indications point
at biases) spice and it will stink

as will most agendas

to acquire a taste for delicacy anyone can acquire, even for taste of Barnum's
Fejee Mermaid (thousands came), the advertised *wonderful specimen
of creation* (thank God for that), that had, Barnum conceded,

died in great agony, true, true, the agony

of the baboon that supplied the mermaid's head, of the orangutan that supplied
breasts, shoulders, arms (most of the maternal signature), agony
of the unspecified fish's body and tail, agony of the faith mourning and marveling

at the one corpse of its kind: the only mistake, God's daughter
instead of his son. Pandora with a box between her legs she had to open,
that is what boxes are for, and because of that, we're here, manipulating

identical twins into births generations apart; here: a woman has eight embryos
unsuccessfully implanted, and some move beyond mere dreaming of reviving
the DNA of their heroes thinking the lived life a promise of the life to be lived,

as if they will be dictators for their heroes and heroics can never dull or pale, ears
on the back of a white rat whereas fantasy let four rats become the four horses
that pull Cinderella's coach until midnight when the four horses become

apocalyptic. Every generation loses something

but as long as this loss makes it possible to gain something else,
to sidestep as though really traveling to galaxies more distant
than distance where some believe we can witness

life beginning in nutrient-laden watery primordial soup just starting
to diversify, mutate as we know life does because we're here, each one of us
the result   and it's okay to call it intelligent or miraculous no matter

what it really is.

—in memory of Amy Clampitt

ADVICE

Do not write about the Holocaust
young sable lady; some subjects must be earned
not dreamed; they are dishonored
by the imagination where they become forgeries,
trivialities, insults

so stay out of that region of abjection;
you have misery a-plenty in your zone, that is your first
assignment: your upheaval, your disadvantage and disgrace, your
own humiliation is sufficient; don't think this
the only sadness; don't respond so quickly

to the great shadow of it that you make a universal cloud
you must deal with because all shadows that meet, merge;
you have not yet done well with the small ineptitudes
of men, the poisoning of a single glass of water
someone you no longer care to love—for you could,
a human being may love anyone—gulps in the middle
of the night; any waking, you see, during the night

is in the middle: we get no further than half-way through difficulty;
for all its certainty, an end is unseen, and everything announces certainty
of descent into your own messes; there is no need to shop
for enormous horror in a Europe you haven't seen, when on your sleeve
is a not-so-innocent flower (it does allow itself to be penetrated by bees)
not quite so yellow as the stars with their *Juden*; what do you know

but a name-tag at a conference at which you are proud to be panelist, key-note
speaker enticing an audience to laughter that does not resound
beyond the auditorium and the four-star accommodations
where three times a day you call room-service requesting delicacies,
the white linen napkin snapping into place in that lap of luxury
you repeatedly deny, although look, it is continuously occupied,
right now
with a lap-top computer, right now

ξ

When I got the advice, I took it seriously, but in fact
it offended me, and I'm no longer afraid to say so, how I resented
his assumptions that I could not be justified
in becoming another echo of lamentation, surrounding myself
with vespers as impossible as silk
that falls from my body without my feeling it, without
my knowing it, this unintentional sloughing of hope
that seems weightless yet the filaments

of webbing are so tough that if someone ever manages to copy products of
spiders and worms on our large distorted human scale, we will have
invincible fiber that I hope is in the right hands, that the benevolent don't jettison
thinking it too frail, thinking this silkenness just another flimsy belief.
I had wanted
to take silk with me into the shower; I had believed it
to be my skin; I have to take with me everything anytime I travel,
from room to room, I clutch my wedding photos, my young child's pale
blue stuffed hippopotamus, the notebook of my earliest stories, the ones
that survived my minor miseries and inelegances, for all did not,

my favorite, the one most handled about vampires for whom
there were blood clouds, blood wells, blood lozenges (I ate Ludens like
candy since Ludens was allowed and Feen-a-mint, the laxative gum),
blood markets where farmers sold their blood turnips and blood fruit
that the young could suck in their carriages and that supported
suitable blood cake to celebrate each neckless year; the candles
were like veins on fire.

ξ

Professor, this poem is not revenge,
it is forgiveness
for that is what everyone needs.

ξ

In file, march to a discretionary hand, you left,
you right, you—still so muscled, you have hoarded food,
committed gluttony, and now you look heroic, you

100

can be bribed, you will live to tell all but the truth
for you traded conscience for food and I wish
for the same opportunity—you suffer mistakes
when Herr Doktor has to fuss with flies, all kinds,
and an itch more unbearable than these choices,
than the music to this, stirrings in the heart
as something loved goes in another direction.

Professor, did I tell you, Sir, that the adults who loved me
while my parents worked were Jews displaced from Dresden
who had only me for sparkle, only me
for holidays? Did I tell you that I'm descended

from their memories, nights when all
they had was fog? Should I have to tell you,
to prove my rights to witness, care, to replace

silk with the best I can offer, these words
pulled from places within me that my husband
and his powerful fucking can't reach or rock?
The world's computers are linked; at 2 a.m.

I visit shrines all over Europe and Asia; when
D. C.'s Holocaust Memorial Museum opened, I was there
feeling uneasy about my innocence for innocence
can not actually be proven; it is becoming increasingly
difficult to prove because we are finally learning our hearts.

Now I beg for logic, the precursor to mercy.

As I beg for logic, the precursor to mercy,
my hands touch every part of my body
that they can, looking for what was valued
this strange moment   of selection.   What sparkle
in me makes him choose me to come to him
as if my virginity were an ignorance
I would appreciate his exposing
so that I might be ashamed, instead, of not knowing him
as he can be naked, as if flesh is necessarily gentle
and the irritation of his wool is not irritation
wool learned from the skin it rubbed.

101

He has an office. I am afraid
of its tidiness;
he is too   so I am invited
each Tuesday so that he may know exactly why
he feels so much like repenting
in me, but I can't absorb his wrong; it trickles
down my legs, the only trickle, I don't menstruate
since no longer am I a woman; when he
is with me, I know for sure that I am no longer
a woman.
                    He has longed for a beast and finding none

lowered his standards to the lovely nothing
I was until coming here *I could be more beast*
        than Lizzie Borden dreaming in Sunday school (my province, Sir)
        of wildness.   It is called the beating of wings,
        it is assignment of brutality to grace.

        I think so long as comets orbit, their tails away
        from the sun that it is wise to shrink from brightness,
        to duck from the blast called day

        and choose to wait for searchlights, the beams
        that something could bend into halos if this light weren't tethered,
        without orbit, just swaying,   responding like Geiger counter
        needles incredibly obedient and aroused by the presence
        of Roentgen units, rads.   These changes, these degenerations

        of body are the same choices the body makes in response
        to chemotherapy or to the teen girl's bringing a brush dipped
        in radium   to a point   with her tongue and lips, her job during the war,
        then painting on wristwatches numbers that glow in darkness,
        the radium in her stomach glowing there, fame of Madame Curie
        incubating there   and in hot spots in her throat, mouth
        and breasts,   think romance,   luminous lymph
        remember she supported herself well, miraculously
        becoming hostess to tribes of tumors from painting twelve
        disciples of time on the clock face.   Tonight, in this hot spot

I choose goodness, to him or to my mother coming
out the chimney in all her rage at what I do with him

all the blessings spilled on the floor, luggage and spectacles, hair
and shoes, his boots, iron cross and belt, my rags almost off
always as if I don't give a damn about blessings.   But I do

> *especially those with their tails away from the sun,*
> *their ice melting, gas escaping, orbit deteriorating, cold dust settling*
> *although a tail a hundred million miles long seemed long enough*
> *to protect them.*   Only because I must   I too burn up

in such atmosphere.

ξ

Mine was not the only *A*

                                        and I will not abandon this poem
that attempts to touch much of what keeps touching me
                    shaping me into a woman who hopes to finish knowing herself
in time to begin to know something else.

NOT SUFFERING

Why is it that I no longer suffer? Have reasons stopped, benefits—especially
for artists? Is it just that by virtue of our carbon, we all have diamonded souls,
every little Tutsi and Hutu?

What hurts is not changing, so I adjust, say it's mere matter of perspective
although that's addiction to optimism as once I was addicted to God

—I've just changed my mind, been changed by my mind.

No longer, for instance, do I need to make Cleopatra VII black, the African half of African-
American, not that a powerful woman would mind what she's called—even enemy
to Rome—so long as it not disrupt her state of mind, not that, given the Ptolemaic bouts
of incest and sibling rivalry, the state

of her mind should be held so trustworthy. Really, it's Elizabeth Taylor's state of mind
(more so than Colbert's) that warped the actual modesty of the role, modesty Shakespeare
was hard put to avoid, unimpressed with empires and disliking crowns for not
having to work at their faithfulness, but the language now assumes

regality and pomp not necessarily there when it was written; but so daunting
beside the ungraciousness with which we take inventory of the world, the little pieces
adding up the way mountains

are the sum of molehills, the way that basic arithmetic still is
the remedy of choice for problems.

The necessity simply escapes me, the benefit of insisting this woman be black (or anything
else)—Mark Antony and Julius Caesar (who may have been sterile although Cleopatra
was wise enough to become pregnant with a child that claimed Caesar) would be no more
available, as if without her, black women of this continent

have no notable identity, but is she really so important, whether or not she was a murderer?
Must we clamor to descend from queens more notorious than gracious? A whole talk show in
the seventies arguing whether or not, as the dyed-red headed author claimed, Cleopatra was a
strawberry blonde. *She was Egyptian, Honey; you know, walk, talk like an Egyptian—Blonde
and out of Africa? I don't think so.* What are we

if we do not claim her, if her rumored eyes today spark pity instead of grandeur?
—for we've seen them only helpless in the Praise The Lord Club when Tammy Faye
put all her optimism in them and they were just targets

for derision, Tammy Faye, with brass (exaggerated gold) faucets if not barges,
whose Jim, the closest to the circles she painted on, circles
most women deny and try to conceal because of battered acquisition,

was unimpressed with her efforts
so he slept with Jessica, young, pretty with the no make-up look
of serious make-up, tricks that are the reputation of Cleopatra no matter
what truth there is to contrast, truth's only function, to distinguish itself from all else,
something Tammy Faye and Cleopatra both do. And that appeals, what we call

independence, the same as what we call Hurston's Janie who was a southern Cleopatra
with a slave or two in her ancestry, with raven-smooth hair long as asps and skin without
melanin handicap if handicap is what that is, independence afforded Janie because her beauty
could not be contested in any context, like the first black Miss America and long

before that, you doubters, that black, tar-black (virtually) Miss Universe (when Vanessa
Williams was still innocent), from Trinidad and Tobago, so stunning, the audience gasped,
that breath poised to become the first note of a perfect aria named Janelle Commissiong
to whom, when she first walked out in the parade of countries, was immediately handed the
crown and scepter—who could compete?—she wasn't free of the darkness and kink too
many can't accept in themselves, suffering needlessly; it's just color and color
does the peacock grand and the sunsets and the storms and is the most trusted sign
of spring. Cleopatra

had no Jesus (and had even less in George Bernard Shaw's account) yet lack alone is not
suffering that can happen amidst inundation, her head on coins that subjects needing (not
suffering) to see themselves in the queen could use as mirrors. Did, though; didn't

the Egyptian servants tend to be darker? Is it possible that painting black pictures even
in Cleo's day (for she was dark, gypsy to Shakespeare, according to tall-dark-and-
handsome's meaning olive—white for all practical purposes, but such purposes
are the ones most resistible) was not rewarded, for the result is *Guernica,*

or outer space too cold and empty to suffer
being all there is to link everything, being all there is to navigate

and yet this blackness really is what the novices with metaphors say: canvas
for a universe that is not finished on which Cleopatra is painted, a star living longer
than anything else then also dying yet still can not be said to be suffering

for dying releases grief that often has no other release
and it can be so still, so removed from any other offenses, slow and elegant

in a procession of cars whose little flags are a more effective patriotism, for all yield
to the slow occasion, the progress of freight; in death

we each stop traffic, run red lights and stop signs without penalty, expected,
in fact, to dispense with laws, for laws are subordinate to grief; how beautiful
when law bends and it becomes hard not to see grace in it, road hogs

experiencing their yielding as if they are what we say lambs
were meant to be while grief controls the streets, moves at the pace

we need to travel in order to appreciate the journey.
And though as slow as snails don't know they are

the funeral flags still flutter, not suffering for this blatant unoriginality—you know,
the rhythm of heartbeats, beating wings of hummingbirds, butterflies, luna moths, leaves:

so true nothing else is worth saying
but then for saying it, being accused of not saying enough.

ACCESSIBLE HEAVEN

You remember being bathed,
surrendering pink soap
to someone who trusts that your dirt
won't adhere to her own skin.
In a minute a rag is lost to lather.

Terry nubs like taste buds
savor your back and thighs, summoning,
from the six-inch wet depth, your glory.
On the surface of opaque water
is the white conquest of suds
unsullied by what supports their voyage.

You want to watch it forever, risk
pneumonia and croup
just so your hand can be the flotilla's
dark sail. Then her hand
activates the drain, and the holiness
leaves in a vortex.

Not one to spoil you,
she grabs a towel, frisks you,
rubs off everything but the clean
that stays with you
all afternoon.

EPILOGUE

THE LIGHTER SIDE OF
SHADOWS OF MONSTERS

Snow makes it seem too easy, this cascading,
this white delight in freefall as if uninfluenced
coming into the world, traveling ruined atmosphere.

Late in April, branches and grass, even the tansy ragwort,
are smothered in the cold finery of second chance, unexpected
and innocent beginning.
It is the right of snow
that falls on democracy to do this, force
a pristine transformation on areas of nastier ambition.

For the moment it looks as if the world is made of scrapings
from the cheek of an old wife who has practiced
all her years trust and faith, whose tales either begin
or end with snow, for that is the way of wisdom, a struggle
to catch it on the tongue and taste it before it melts
into water I already know.

But it is not the hope of snow; rather it is snow fortifying
into banks, tires churning it brown and troublesome
as complexion that reassures and rescues.
I take my cues from snow succeeding in descent,
though only to melt in jars and pitchers old wives fill
or to be tramped tight as the abdominals of a boxer
in his glory that isn't necessarily white or icy.

Did you know, an old wife asks, handing me some, *that
there are wasp heads in Fig Newtons?*
As soon as the blizzard relents, I won't have to listen
or care, but for now the crunch of the Newtons is good,
necessary, sensual, especially an idea of wasps, my swallowing
their stingers, then in a few weeks swallowing embroidery needles
and crochet hooks on the way to swords, or maybe no further
than Wilkinson Sword razor blades if the point is only danger
and the unlikeliness of recognition.

Every generation of snowmen is doomed
yet they are harder to pity than the monsters
of Drs. Frankenstein and Moreau. Here's to the lighter side
of the shadows of monsters, those beautiful snow angels
that grow ragged in rising temperature and sun.

Notes

The italicized phrase "the most pure and white starch" in "Those Who Love Bones" was quoted from *The History and Folklore of North American Wildflowers* by Timothy Coffey. Facts about the status of Joseph Merrick's bones were derived from *Dead Men Do Tell Tales* by William R. Maples.

In "Juniper Tree" by the Brothers Grimm, on which "Juniper Tree of Knowledge" is based, Marie (sometimes known as Ann Marie) is the biological child of the second wife and her new husband, making Marie and John half siblings, but I have borrowed the more frequent fairy tale approach to remarriage (as in "Cinderella" and "Hansel and Gretel") in which second wives do not have children with their new husbands. This lack of procreational link usually leads to tension in the tales as the threat of biological inheritance (the man will have children from his first marriage) emphasizes the second wife's tenuous position in the household. Furthermore, the second wife's behavior is far more consistent with the depiction of step-mothers; biological mothers usually retain virtue, dying (as in "Snow White") before they must compete with their daughters, a competition reserved for step-mothers who are bitter and generally older than the youthful first wife; in fact, they are approaching or have entered menopause and therefore have little chance of conceiving a child that can compete effectively with her husband's children. Finally, there was greater potential for love to blossom between them if the brother and sister were not biologically linked, so I have left to them an avenue for uncomplicated romantic love should they desire to live happily ever after.

"Soft construction with boiled beans," an italicized phrase in part 2 of "Last Chance for the Tarzan Holler" is the alternate title for the Dali painting "Premonition of Civil War."

The italicized passages in "Ear" are quoted from *The Sex Life of Flowers* by Bastiaan Meeuse and Sean Morris.

The photograph referred to in "The Right Empowerment of Light" is "Backlit Radishes" by Linda Butler.

In "For Hagar," italicized biblical passages were taken from Genesis 16:5, 7-12 in the Jerusalem Bible, Genesis 17:20-1, 21:10, and Genesis 25:12-18 of the Revised Standard Version. It should

114

be noted that Esau, elder twin, in fact is designated loser. From Isaac, who had given Jacob the full extent of his blessing, Esau received a consolation prize that wasn't particularly conciliatory: *Far from the richness of the earth shall be your dwelling-place, far from the dew that falls from heaven. You shall live by your sword, and you shall serve your brother.* (Genesis 27:39-40, Jerusalem Bible). Esau is essentially cursed and, understandably, vows to kill Jacob. Not all of the italicized passages in this poem are biblical quotes.

Although in "Crystals," the implication is that Anarcha, her actual name, was or had been pregnant, there is not yet evidence of her pregnancies, suggesting that her fistula had some other cause, such as horseback riding. However, among those multiparas, especially enslaved multiparas, who develop these fistulas, repeated childbirth is often the cause.

"A Walk through the *Dark Embrace*" is a series of poems based upon an exhibit at the University of Michigan Art Museum in March 1996 called: "Dark Embrace: Images of War, Death, and the Apocalypse." Additional details and facts were derived from *The Bestiary of Christ,* by Louis Charbonneau-Lassay, translated by D. M. Dooling.

Italicized lines about partridges in "Ode to the Cat-headed Consort in a Painting by Bosch" are taken from *The Book of Beasts*, translated and edited by T. H. White. The poem responds to a detail of one of the panels of "The Temptation of Saint Anthony" by Hieronymous Bosch.

In "Sour Milk," the quotes on P. T. Barnum are from *P. T. Barnum, America's Greatest Showman,* by Philip B. Kunhardt, Jr.; Philip B. Kunhardt III, and Peter W. Kunhardt.

Elizabeth Alexander is a poet whose first book is built around the title poem: *Venus Hottentot.* While Alexander does not own the life of the woman called *Hottentot Venus,* an alias for Sarah Bartmann, I can no longer think of the *Hottentot Venus* without also thinking of Alexander's poem (such is its impact), so therefore, I give honor to her poem.

"Sour Milk" also contains a line from *Oh What a Beautiful Morning,* from the musical *Oklahoma.*

"Sour Milk" is dedicated to the memory of Amy Clampitt, not because this poem has anything to do with her preoccupations, but as my poem began to behave much as the event horizon of a black hole, pulling all of the available into its composition, warping the surrounding space, and allowing nothing that entered it to escape, I was much reminded of Amy Clampitt's poems' grand gestures, the encyclopedic demands her poems exert, her tremendous viral stanzas in which language swirls. I am thankful for her body of work and the presence it maintains long after the demise of the corporeal.

On "Not Suffering": Janie, the protagonist in Zora Neale Hurston's *Their Eyes Were Watching God* is every bit the independent black woman I was taught she was, but not enough credit has been given to her independence's primary sponsors: Janie's exceptionally long (below the waist and real), smooth-textured hair and pale complexion that community consensus decrees are to be prized above coarser and darker varieties. For instance, upon the death of her second husband, before Janie greets the public to announce the death of the town's dignitary, Janie pauses to remove the headrag (that her husband required so that her superiority [hair] would not threaten [emasculate] him), drawing strength from even longer hair, commenting to her reflection, that she unashamedly finds pleasing, that *mah glory was still there*. She does not pretend not to be aware of her beauty; confidently wearing the overalls of a farmer, she can't hide her shape. Thus empowered, Janie faces the public and pursues the love of her life, a much younger man, who on their first date rushes, not to undress her, but to comb her hair; in fact, he has brought a comb with him just for this purpose. Recognizing power, he acquiesces, enjoying the sexual generosity (that no one else has) that results from her victory. Would a generous dose of melanin and nappiness bring Janie to ruin? Could she as successfully exert her independence had she been endowed with only the most ordinary equipment? Early in this century, perhaps the belief that only black women like Janie could promote themselves (or would be promoted by the majority) was genuine, but now, more is required. And it is up to each woman who is not Janie (or her super model, celebrity equivalent of any skin tone) to require that more of herself.

The actual coloring of the Miss Universe from Trinidad and Tobago, Janelle Commissiong, was more like the bark, when it is wet, of the crab apple tree in my yard; not tar black, of course, but rich, and incredibly dark, a velvety chocolate Hershey and Nestlé know nothing about, and even darker when I darkened the images on the television; didn't you do that too sometimes?—just turn that brightness knob, and all the Miss America contestants are black. I used to do that, oh years and years ago. Now, I don't much care about the pageants or my power over them, but I'm glad I know how that power once made me feel.

It was actually Jill Rosser and not an old wife who informed me about the likelihood of wasp heads in Fig Newtons in "The Lighter Side of Shadows of Monsters."

About the Author

THYLIAS MOSS is the author of six volumes of poetry, a memoir, and a book for children. Her second collection of poetry was shortlisted for the National Book Critics Circle Award and her fourth won the National Poetry Series Open Competition. A 1996 MacArthur Fellow, she is also the recipient of a Guggenheim Felowship, a Whiting Writer's Award, and the Witter Bynner Prize. Married and raising two sons in Ann Arbor, she teaches at the University of Michigan.